FIND YOUR WORKVERSE

Gen Z's Playbook to
Thrive at Work. With AI.
With Humans. With Purpose.

Michelle Duval & Dan Negroni
With Coach Marlee

marlee

First published in 2025 by Marlee Australia Pty Ltd
Marlee.com

Text copyright © Marlee Australia Pty Ltd, 2025.
Authors: Michelle Duval and Dan Negroni, with contributions from "Coach Marlee," an AI developed by Marlee Australia Pty Ltd.
Moral rights: Michelle Duval and Dan Negroni assert their moral rights to be identified as authors.

Design and typography copyright © Marlee Australia Pty Ltd, 2025. All rights reserved.

This book is protected by the Copyright Act 1968. No part may be reproduced, stored, or shared in any form without written permission from the publisher, except as permitted under the Act or for brief quotations with proper credit.

Please send all permission queries to: Marlee Australia Pty Ltd, 377 Kent Street, Suite #1058, Sydney, NSW 2000, or hello@getmarlee.com

A catalogue record for this book is available from the National Library of Australia

ISBN: 978-1-7641184-3-9 (paperback – updated edition)
ISBN: 978-1-7641184-2-2 (hardcover)
ISBN: 978-1-7641184-0-8 (ebook)
ISBN: 978-1-7641184-6-0 (audiobook)

Cover and internal design: Alexandra Andrieș and Jon Whitby
Publisher: Marlee Australia Pty Ltd
Development Editor: Emily Willis
Proofreader: Alyssa Kruse

The information in this book is published in good faith and for general information purposes only. Although the authors and publisher believe at the time of going to press that the information is accurate, they do not assume and hereby disclaim any liability to any party for loss, damage, or disruption caused by errors or omissions, whether they result from negligence, accident, or any other cause.

Marlee acknowledges the Traditional Owners of Country throughout Australia and their continuing connection to lands, waters, and communities. We pay our respects to the people, the cultures, and the Elders past and present, and extend that respect to Indigenous peoples on whose lands we live and work around the world.

The word Marlee derives from the Gathang word Maali (Maa – li), which refers to the native Elderberry tree on Birrbay Country (Mid-North Coast, NSW, Australia). Maali comes from the Gathang language, spoken by the Birrbay, Warrimay, and Guringay peoples, and refers to the placename *Marlee* on Birrbay Country, where you can expect to find the Elderberry tree. Using the original language of place tells us important things about Country and kin. *Maali* represents transformation, growth, and healing for the Birrbay people.

The Birrbay people have granted Marlee the right to publish a translation of Maali from the Gathang language in accordance with the Indigenous Cultural Intellectual Property Statement.

To our Gen Z children, students, teammates, and coachees.
You shared your stories with courage.
You spoke your truths with honesty.
You asked questions that mattered.
This book exists because of you, and for you.
It's been a privilege to listen.

When you read this book, you're not alone.

You have an AI teammate called Marlee.

Use this QR code to bring your Workverse fully to life, for *you*.

Reading this book alone will inspire you and give you tools. Working with your AI teammate, Marlee, can change your life.

Marlee.com/workverse

Roadmap to Your Workverse

You Made It! So, Let's Go!	XIII
This is Your Workverse Playbook	XV
How We Wrote Your Playbook	XVII
How to Use This Book: Your Roadmap to the Workverse	XIX

PART 1
YOUR NEW WORKVERSE

CHAPTER 1

You're in the Right Place: You Are the Future of Work	3
💡 Bring your future to life, one day at a time	7

CHAPTER 2

AI and You and the Revolutionary Impact on Work	15
💡 Your edge: Trace the tech that shaped you	27

CHAPTER 3

Redefining Career and Workverse: 2035 Starts with You!	31
💡 Now build your human skills map	50

CHAPTER 4

Gen Z's Opportunity:
Your Next Step and Roles You'll Create 55

  💡 *Discover the roles that light you up* 71

CHAPTER 5

Navigating the Risks Ahead Your Way 87

  💡 *Build your resilience toolkit* 115

PART 2
FINDING YOUR PLACE IN THE WORKVERSE

CHAPTER 6

The Gen Z Superpower Sweet Spot 123

  💡 *Explore your Gen Z edge* 133

CHAPTER 7

Play to Your Personal Strengths 137

  💡 *Use your results to play to your strengths* 148

CHAPTER 8

Create and Build Your Path 151

  💡 *Match your motivations to work environments* 163

CHAPTER 9

Land Your Dream Job Now 167

  💡 *Make finding a job your job* 168

CHAPTER 10

Go Grow Yourself   193

💡 *Your growth roadmap: Small shifts, big impact*   208

CHAPTER 11

Crack the Collaboration Code   215

💡 *Build a team that clicks*   234

PART 3
UNLOCK YOUR PEAK POTENTIAL

CHAPTER 12

Mastering Your Flow   241

💡 *Realign your work with what energizes you*   258

CHAPTER 13

Hack Your Productivity   267

💡 *Your personalized productivity stack*   282

CHAPTER 14

Step Up and Lead: Closing the Leadership Gap   289

💡 *Shape your personal leadership path*   301

CHAPTER 15

Build Your Life with Real Meaning   305

💡 *Start mapping: Your life, your rhythm*   311

CHAPTER 16

Empower Gen Z to Thrive: A Guide for Evangelists   333

💡 *Your 90-day support plan: Help Gen Z thrive*   337

ENDNOTES

We'll See You in the Workverse   348

Acknowledgments   351

About the Authors   353

About *The Gen Z at Work Study*   356

Endnotes   357

You Made It! So, Let's Go!

Before you jump in, pause for a sec. Breathe. Tap into *you*.

Think about what you want to get out of this book.

Need a jumpstart? Here's what some early explorers said they were here for:

- Finally, no longer second-guessing every decision
- Finding my next step when the future felt overwhelming
- Spotting my strengths *and* my blind spots
- Boosting my confidence
- Scoring that dream role
- Creating a work vibe I actually believe in
- Leveling up my focus and getting stuff done
- Growing *without* hitting burnout
- Not letting tough feedback hurt me
- Stopping awkward convos before they turn into conflict

There's no one-size-fits-all. Just what matters most to *you*! Let's help you figure it out, together.

This is Your Workverse Playbook

This isn't a step-by-step career manual. It's your space to explore how you work, what drives you, and where you want to make a real impact. Inside, you'll find *you* by diving into the biggest shifts shaping work in 2035, unlocking your strengths, building new skills, adapting fast, and teaming up with AI to make it happen. This is about your lifelong creation of a work life you can own.

This playbook is here to help you double down on your superpowers and shape the future, not just survive it.

We wrote this for you.

We wrote this as a playbook because, after coaching thousands through career changes, burnout, leadership struggles, and future-of-work shifts, we kept hearing the same thing from Gen Z:

> "I know what I care about, but I don't know how to turn it into work that actually sustains me."

If you've ever felt that way, you're not alone, and that's exactly why we wrote Workverse.

You're navigating the *Workverse*—a work world that demands purpose, performance, and constant reinvention, all while you're trying to stay mentally well. We're not here to add pressure. We're here to help you tap into what energizes you and build from there.

We studied what really drives Gen Z at work, connected with thousands of 16–28-year-olds, built an app to support you and your teams, and wrote this book—all distilled so you can put it to use straight away.

We created this playbook to help you:

- Harness our Gen Z research and hyper-personalize it—for your work today and your next steps.
- Stay energized by designing work that fits how you're wired
- Find and shape your own path in a world of evolving roles
- Turn your strengths into influence, momentum, and growth
- Learn to work *with* AI, not against it
- Make confident choices without burning out or selling out

Before we show you how we wrote this playbook, here's why it matters: knowing where these insights come from helps you trust them—and actually use them.

How We Wrote Your Playbook

We'll keep this quick. (Promise.)

Our journey began in 2001 with a bold question: *What truly motivates people at work, and what drives their success?* When we published our research, *Unlocking Gen Z at Work: A Generational Impact Study*, in late 2024, it became clear that Gen Z isn't just unique—you're re-architecting the workplace.

This book is powered by insights from that global study:

- 395,000+ people (80,000+ Gen Z—more than one in five contributors)
- 159 countries
- The largest database of motivational traits at work ever collected

It's a true and representative snapshot of how your generation works—what motivates you, your strengths, how you communicate, make decisions, and the kind of environments where you thrive. These insights come from Marlee's *Motivation Analysis*—the same tool you can try anytime at Marlee.com, giving us a deep, data-driven understanding of what sets Gen Z apart.

We combined this with coaching insights and predictive AI to shape every chapter around what actually works.

Gen Z has strengths that no other generation has had at its fingertips. Your digital agility, social consciousness, and hunger for purpose are exactly what the future of work needs. You have a once-in-a-generation opportunity to define work on your terms and help solve the complex challenges we face today.

Throughout, we'll refer to these findings as *The Gen Z at Work Study*. This isn't theory, the usual BS Gen Z stereotypes or nonsense published in the media—it's your field guide to thriving in the Workverse, on your own terms.

How to Use This Book: Your Roadmap to the Workverse

We know by now you're probably thinking, *Okay, but how do I approach this book so I can get the most out of it?* That's a great question! Let us break it down for you.

The book is written in three sections as a guide to your personal journey.

Part 1: Your new Workverse

The world you're stepping into. Explore what will be changing in work by 2035—from AI teammates and task-based roles to climate innovation and borderless teams—and why Gen Z is uniquely positioned to lead.

Part 2: Finding your place in the Workverse

Where it gets personal. Dig into your unique work style, motivations, and strengths, and map the path that's right for you.

Part 3: Unlock your peak potential

Time to apply it all. Practical tools to help you flow, thrive, and stay grounded, even when things get intense.

Here's how each chapter works

To keep things simple and actionable, every chapter follows the same rhythm:

 **New Workverse reality:** Your quick download on what's shifting in work, from new roles and skills to real data from *The Gen Z at Work Study*.

 **Your productivity edge:** Where you'll get hands-on. You'll try coaching practices, reflection prompts, and tools to build your own playbook.

 **Create real impact:** Each chapter wraps with clear actions you can take, right now or in the future, to make it stick and move forward with momentum.

Your hyper-personalized growth system

 All through this playbook, you'll see **Marlee moments**—little nudges that connect what you're reading to what drives **you**. Because it's not enough to just know the insights. Gen Z's biggest edge is in how you apply them ***personally***.

That's where Marlee comes in. Marlee's technology helps you **discover your unique motivations**: the patterns that explain why some tasks fire you up and others drain you. These motivations are the key to your energy, confidence, and growth. When you understand them, you can design work that actually fits you, so you stop wasting energy and start building momentum.

And it's free. No catch. Just your growth OS: this book + Marlee. Together, they give you a system you can use right now in your work, whether that's figuring out your next step after school, finding your place in a new role, or building a work life you love.

Don't let this stay theory. Jump into Marlee.com, uncover personal insights, and take them with pride to work. That's how you'll unlock your unique superpowers and keep growing long after you've turned the last page.

Ready? Let's build your Workverse, your way!

Part 1
Your New Workverse

The future isn't some sci-fi flick; it's already streaming live, and you're cast in the starring role. In this section, we'll lift the lid on what's changing at work, why it matters, and how you can shape what's next.

CHAPTER 1
You're in the Right Place: You Are the Future of Work

The world is experiencing an unprecedented revolution at work. It started with dramatic changes during the COVID pandemic, and now AI is reshaping how we live and work. And it's doing so at a pace that no generation has ever experienced before.

While AI is a key driver, work is also rapidly changing due to *you* and *your generation*. The cultural shifts born and led from within your generation are facilitating, and in some cases, demanding a deep rethink and evolution in the way we work. You are the pioneers; you are the future of work.

Some of you have already taken bold steps. You've built businesses from bedrooms, created brands between lectures, and sparked movements from schoolyards or TikTok feeds. Remember when 15-year-old Greta Thunberg stood outside Swedish Parliament with a cardboard sign? She didn't have a media team. She had guts. And you amplified her voice until the world had to listen.

But not all leadership makes headlines, and it doesn't need to. Maybe your boldest move so far has been switching majors when the old path didn't feel right. Or being the first in your family to graduate. Or showing up for a shift when you felt anxious but didn't want to let your team down. Maybe it was raising your hand in class when no one else would or standing up for a friend when it was easier to stay quiet. These choices may look small, but they're how empathy and resilience take root.

And resilience has always been at the heart of shaping the future. For generations, Indigenous and First Nations peoples across the world have shown us what it means to build communities grounded in strength, purpose, and connection to land and culture.

You've made mental health something we can finally talk about. Therapy moved out of the shadows and into the norm. Creators taught breathing techniques in 30 seconds, and you didn't just watch. You shared them, tried them, and said, "This helped me."

You've launched Etsy shops, built tutoring businesses from your living rooms, designed memes that shaped how millions see the world, and yes, you've also taught your parents how to use half the apps they now rely on. No roadmap. Just curiosity, courage, and community.

And when AI dropped in? While others panicked, you opened a tab. You tested, prompted, built, shared. You didn't sit there asking, *What's going to happen to me?* You were already asking, *What can I create with this?*

But we know none of this has been easy.

You've grown up as the ground kept shifting. Recession, pandemic, climate anxiety, constant change. You've changed majors, changed plans, questioned everything, even yourself. You've pushed through burnout, self-doubt, and uncertainty. Some of you are still figuring out what you're good at or wondering if you'll ever feel certain about anything.

And yet, you keep showing up. You keep learning. Creating. Asking the hard questions. That takes grit. That's growth in real time.

That instinct, that "try it, break it, remix it" mindset, is your edge. And now it's time to make it intentional.

Because this next focus, this next season of work, is about building your own Workverse.

And the Workverse isn't a straight ladder or a corner office. It's fast, flexible, and agile. It's AI-powered, people-powered, and purpose-fueled. It runs on clarity, not conformity.

You've got reach. The pivots you've made, the setbacks you've survived, the experiments you've run—that wasn't lost time. That was training.

So now the question is: what will you do with that reach?

This playbook is here to help you own who you already are. It's a system to help you lead with your strengths, stay energized, collaborate with both humans and AI, and grow in ways that *actually feel right to you.*

You've already been doing the hardest part: showing up, trying, learning out loud, starting again, and lifting each other up.

Now it's time to focus that momentum. Aim it. Scale it.

Gen Z is shaping the future. You're resetting the standard, not just for yourselves, but for everyone who comes next.

You're raising the bar for what work can feel and be like. You're proving that leadership can be more human. That small acts can spark big impact. That purpose and performance can actually work together.

What will you do with this level of potential impact? How will you shape your future? How will you help the generations that come after you shape theirs?

We're here to help you find your unique piece of the puzzle, your *through line*, and to help you own it and crush it.

Let's go!

Bring your future to life, one day at a time

Design your ideal workday

You've just explored one of the biggest turning points in modern work history: a future of work rebuilt not on ladders or corner offices, but on something far more powerful: your energy, your values, your purpose, and your ability to work with technology in a deeply human way.

Now it's time to bring that vision a little closer. What does it actually look like when your work life is shaped by how you are wired to thrive?

Before you start thinking about what's next, take a moment.

The most powerful way to prepare for what's ahead isn't guessing what job might exist in 2035. It's by getting radically clear on what energizes you and how you want to experience your work life, from the inside out.

This is about designing a day that feels real, fulfilling, and unmistakably *you*.

Step 1: Envision your ideal workday

To start, give yourself a moment to reflect. This is your chance to imagine a workday that truly energizes you. You might want to write it out, record a voice memo, or even sketch it visually on a whiteboard: whatever helps you bring your future to life.

Imagine it's 2035, and you've just wrapped up a full day of work that left you feeling energized and fulfilled. Describe your day from start to finish in rich detail.

Here are some prompts to get you started:

- What time do you wake up? Where are you living?
- Do you work from home, a company office, a creative hub, a café on another continent, or a little of everything?
- What kind of work are you doing? What skills are you using?
- Are you collaborating with people in person, virtually, or through immersive tech?
- What tools, platforms, or AI teammates are part of your routine?
- How do you take breaks? What do you eat? What energizes you at midday?
- Who do you connect with: teammates, clients, communities?
- How do you wrap up your day? What makes you feel proud or content?

Write your 2035 day like a journal entry, no limits, no filters.

_____

_____

_____

_____

_____

_____

_____

_____

Let it flow

Step 2: Spot what energizes you

Now, go back and highlight three to five moments in your imagined day that felt alive, exciting, or deeply meaningful. These are clues to your motivations, not what the world tells you to want, but what actually fuels *you*.

Want to know exactly what energizes you (and what quietly drains you)?

Think of this as your personal energy manual. Here's how to find it:

1. Head to Marlee.com and hit *Start for free*.
2. Take the *Marlee Motivational Analysis* (just once, quick to complete).
3. Click on *Boards* and create your *Individual Results Board*: your personalized snapshot of what fires you up and what wears you down.

You'll uncover things like:

- Do you feel more alive working solo or in a group?
- Do you get a buzz from solving problems in the moment or working toward a long-term goal?
- Do you thrive with structure, or light up with freedom?

Many early readers have said it's like flipping the lights on: suddenly, you can see the patterns behind your energy, focus, and confidence. And with that clarity, you can start designing days that fit you, today and in the future.

> "You don't have to predict the future,
> you just have to imagine the version you'd love to lead,
> and I'll help you start building it from there."
> —**Coach Marlee**

Step 3: Translate vision into action

Choose one energizing element from your vision that you can start exploring *now*.

- Is it a skill? Sign up for a micro-course or start a project.
- Is it a way of working? Experiment with your schedule or try a freelance collaboration.
- Is it a type of impact? Volunteer, build, or join a mission-driven group aligned with that cause.

What's one bold (but doable) move you can make this week to bring a piece of your 2035 Workverse into today?

_____

_____

_____

_____

Step 4: Share it. Shape it. Refine it.

Your 2035 vision isn't static—it's alive. Talk about it with a mentor, a teammate, or even your AI teammate. Let others challenge it, contribute ideas, or help make it even better.

And don't worry if it evolves. That's the point.

> "Clarity isn't a destination, it's a muscle.
> The more you reflect and adjust,
> the stronger your future becomes."
> —Coach Marlee

Your future. Your Workverse. How will you shape it?

> "You have to fight to reach your dream.
> You have to sacrifice and work hard for it."
> —Lionel Messi, Argentinian footballer

By 2035, work will be both radically new and deeply human. But one thing won't change: you are the architect of your own Workverse. Whether you're solving real problems, leading with purpose, collaborating with AI, or mentoring across generations, the power to shape the future starts now.

> "Gen Z has some of the most inclusive, compassionate,
> and thoughtful folk of all generations.
> That's one of the most exciting things about the future."
> —Michelle Duval

To build what's next, we need to understand what's already shifting. Before we dive into future roles, new industries, and bold opportunities ahead, we need to look at the foundations already shifting beneath our feet. The systems you inherited—education, employment, leadership, even the definition of "work"—were built for a different time.

And one of the biggest drivers of that shift is already here. AI isn't on the horizon. It's in your hands. It's not just changing how people work; it's transforming how they learn, create, earn, and lead. And it's moving fast.

That might feel overwhelming. But it's also your greatest advantage. Because Gen Z wasn't just born into disruption, you've been shaping it all along. You're not waiting for permission. You're building, questioning, and creating in real time.

Up next: How to work with AI, not against it, and why it's your most powerful collaborator.

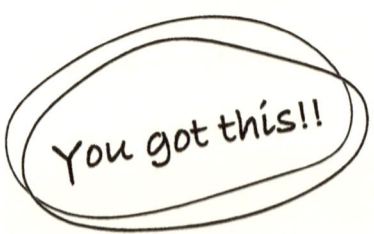

CHAPTER 2

AI and You and the Revolutionary Impact on Work

People + Tech = Magic ★

TL;DR

AI isn't here to replace you; it's here to transform how you work, grow, and lead.

AI moves fast, but what sets you apart is how you combine human strengths with machine speed to shape the future, not just survive it.

- **AI won't likely take jobs, it'll reshape them:** creating new opportunities across every industry.
- **Gen Z is already leading the way:** curious, adaptable, and less tied to outdated systems.
- **AI is a collaborator, not your competitor:** your judgment, creativity, and emotional intelligence are still the edge.
- **New roles are emerging daily:** from regenerative system designers to AI content strategists and beyond.
- **The future of work is regenerative, global, and AI-powered:** you're stepping into it now.

First, what do we mean by AI?

Before we dive into how AI is transforming your work life, let's pause and get clear on what we mean when we say "AI."

For decades, AI lived mostly in research labs. Early versions were rule-based and mathematical: systems that could follow logic or run models, but didn't touch everyday life. Then came the first wave you might remember: Facebook automatically tagging your face in a photo, your iPhone unlocking with just a glance, Netflix learning your taste, or Spotify curating your playlists. In 2016, when Google Translate suddenly stopped sounding robotic and started feeling almost natural, you could feel the shift. AI was no longer a theory; it was part of our daily routine.

The 2020s brought something different: generative AI. This is the wave most people mean today when they say "AI." It doesn't just recognize patterns; it creates: writing essays, drafting emails, designing slides, painting digital art, coding apps, and even producing videos from text prompts. Tools such as ChatGPT, Canva's Magic AI, or Runway can brainstorm, design, or generate on demand.

Alongside this sits predictive AI, which uses patterns in data to forecast what's likely, whether that's predicting role success at work (as Marlee's AI does), mapping future economic shifts, or anticipating what you'll want next.

There are other types of AI, too, like systems that classify data, cluster information, or learn by trial and error, but for your work life right now, generative and predictive AI are the most visible.

All of these fall under what's called Narrow AI: systems built to excel at specific tasks, rather than replicate all of human intelligence.

You'll also hear bigger terms in the conversation: Artificial General Intelligence (AGI), the idea of an AI that could match humans across most cognitive tasks, and Artificial Superintelligence (ASI), a concept of intelligence far beyond human capacity. These raise important ethical questions—from safety to fairness—but they're not currently shaping our daily work life.

For the rest of Workverse, when we say "AI," we mean Narrow AI: the systems you already use and will use more of in your work life. They may not sound futuristic anymore, but they're already powerful enough to transform roles, reshape industries, and open up opportunities no generation has had before you.

> "Pause for a moment: How are you already using AI, maybe without realizing it? From your playlists to your study tools, you've already been using AI for years.
> You're more ready for a future with AI than you think."
> —**Michelle Duval**

Your new Workverse reality: Why AI isn't taking over your job, it's helping you redesign it

By 2030, up to 400 million people could be redesigning their work lives, shifting roles, upskilling, or stepping into industries that don't even exist yet. That's the scale of transformation unfolding as automation and AI reshape what we do and how we do it. And this isn't isolated to a single sector; nearly half of the tasks people are paid to do today could soon be handled by machines.[1]

But AI is just one piece of the puzzle. Global forces like climate change, economic uncertainty, geopolitical tensions, and aging populations are all rewriting the rules of the Workverse. Roles built on routine and repetition are shrinking fast. In their place? A surge in opportunities across green innovation, AI, and data-driven problem-solving. According to the World Economic Forum, it's a massive reset: 92 million jobs displaced, but 170 million new ones created by 2030.[2]

This is a seismic shift. And if you're early in your work life, you're stepping in at the exact moment everything's being rebuilt. Which makes this the perfect time to shape it to fit *you*.

And that future? It's not slowing down to wait. Your ability to learn fast, adapt on the fly, and stay purpose-driven is your biggest competitive advantage.

Even the idea of a "team" is changing. Increasingly, you'll work side by side with AI teammates—tools and platforms that collaborate with you on everything from real-time research, ideation, content creation, and decision-making. Research already shows that AI-assisted teams outperform human-only teams in both speed and outcomes.[3]

You're Gen Z. You're wired for what comes next. AI isn't a threat to your work life; it's a multiplier of your strengths.

Let's explore how

Why Gen Z is wired for this

You're not playing catch-up. You've been growing up alongside this tech.

According to *The Gen Z at Work Study*, you're more motivated by tools and systems than any generation before you. You've got a 66% spike in tech curiosity, and your detail orientation is up 120%, compared to earlier generations. That's a game-changer. It means you're naturally suited to collaborate with AI and spot its blind spots.

> "You're not waiting for permission to try new tools. You just try them. That's rare and powerful."
> —Dan Negroni

And you've got another advantage: high indifference. You're not emotionally attached to outdated systems. You see something that doesn't work, and your first instinct isn't to fix it. It's to ask, *What if we did it completely differently?*

> "I use AI to research, but I don't let it run me.
> It's about knowing when to follow data
> and when to trust your instincts."
> —**Khadijah, 29, marketer**

The tools are just the beginning. What matters most is how you show up, experiment, and grow your skills, especially the ones AI can't replicate.

> "Each shift in technology opens a window.
> The question is: will you see the window,
> and will you step through it?"
> —**Michelle Duval**

It's you + AI, not either/or

AI can crunch the numbers. But it doesn't care about the outcome. It can write you a solid draft, but it won't know if it *feels* right.

That's where you come in. The human voice in the loop. The collaborator who notices nuance, asks better questions, and knows when something's off, even when the data says it's right.

> "Tech without humans being seen, heard, or celebrated is just noise. But together, it's harmony."
> —Dan Negroni

When you blend your empathy, your creativity, and your decision-making with AI's speed and scale, that's when the sparks fly. Think of it like Iron Man's suit: AI enhances your abilities, but it's still you making the critical decisions, setting the vision, and taking action. Just like Tony Stark without the suit is still a genius innovator, you, without AI, still bring creativity, strategy, and human judgment to the table. AI is an amplifier, not a replacement—it's your edge, not your identity.

Here's something that might surprise you: Some of the most successful AI companies operate with surprisingly small teams. The top artificial intelligence startups achieve massive impact with a median of just 89 employees, down from 150 the previous year. These lean, efficient operations raised unprecedented funding at younger ages than ever before.[4]

How did they do it? By pairing bold ideas with AI teammates that cut down on costs, automate the busywork, and supercharge momentum. When tech removes the heavy lifting, small teams can move faster, build smarter, and punch well above their weight.

The acceleration of AI: Faster than any shift before

Every generation has had its "whoa" moment with technology. But this one? It's not a slow evolution—it's a rocket launch.

The printing press took centuries to reshape how humans shared knowledge. Electricity and the internet each needed decades to ripple through homes, workplaces, and industries. But AI is operating on a completely different timeline. Just two years after ChatGPT was released, nearly 40% of US adults between 18 and 64 have already used generative AI, and more than a quarter are using it at work. That pace isn't just fast, it's historically unmatched.[5]

And no one's leaning into it more than Gen Z. Research shows that employees aged 18–29 are the most likely to use AI chatbots at work, far more than earlier generations.[6] You aren't just using AI for admin, you're applying it for ideation, design, analysis, and even coding. That's a massive shift in how quickly new tech is being integrated into daily work.

> "Artificial intelligence, deep learning, machine learning—whatever you're doing if you don't understand it—learn it. Because otherwise, you're going to be a dinosaur within three years."
> —Mark Cuban, entrepreneur and investor

Here's what that feels like: It's not going from early Instagram filters to generative AI content tools; it's more like jumping from riding a bike to co-piloting a spaceship.

> "I feel like every time I learn a new tool,
> there's already something faster.
> It's overwhelming, but also kind of exciting.
> You just have to keep moving." — — →
> —**Tariq, 22, software intern**

If that sounds familiar, you're not alone. And you're probably better at this than you think.

AI has gone global, and it's everywhere

By 2035, AI won't be just chilling in Silicon Valley anymore. It will be embedded in industries you might not expect.

Doctors will rely on AI to map complex treatment plans in real time. Retail teams will use it to predict what you'll need before you even search for it. Creators will collaborate with AI to storyboard videos and generate soundscapes while still shaping the final cut with that human spark.

Every industry, from healthcare to marketing, logistics to sustainability, will see a rise in AI-driven roles. Fields like AI ethics, automation strategy, and AI-powered content creation will explode. The demand for AI specialists will surge, offering new work pathways that didn't exist a decade ago.

> "I was exposed early on to a culture of thinking that every problem in society can be fixed with some sort of computational solution, whether that's a mobile app, a machine-learning model, or some other mechanism to respond to something."
> —Sneha Revanur, "The Greta Thunberg of AI"

That mindset is now global. And it's not about coding everything, it's about reimagining what's possible.

Translation? AI won't replace you. It will make room for you to do what you do best. Like every tech revolution before it, it's set to create entirely new kinds of work.

Lessons from past technological revolutions

There's a myth that new tech wipes out jobs. The truth? It reshapes them and creates entirely new ones. The printing press didn't end writing; it amplified it. It created entirely new roles: typesetters, editors, authors, journalists, and eventually an entire publishing industry. A single innovation sparked thousands of new roles that nobody could have imagined.[7]

The internet didn't end retail; it reshaped how we buy, sell, and even build our brands, sparking new roles such as UX designers, app developers, and yes, even meme consultants. The iPhone took that shift further, catalyzing an app economy that, by 2022, generated more than $1.1 trillion in global sales and now supports more than 2.1 million jobs in the US alone.[8]

Now it's AI's turn, and it's clear: every shift creates a wave of new possibilities. The trick is spotting the opportunity before it becomes the norm.

What might you be doing in 2035?

Let's play this out. Not hypotheticals—real roles, already on the rise. You could be a Regenerative Systems Designer, building circular processes where nothing goes to waste. Or an AI Scriptwriter, co-creating narratives that hit emotional beats and data-driven success metrics. Or maybe you'll be drawn to workforce strategy, where you'll function like a Human Capital Algorithmic Trader, forecasting human potential like a stock portfolio. By 2035, AI will have evolved from a support tool to a strategic collaborator. From AI trainers to Neuro-Interface Designers, roles will blend human expertise with AI-powered decision-making.

You may already be building the skills. Even your side hustle might be more strategic than you realize.

Regenerative work and global teams are just the beginning

By 2035, the most exciting work won't just be *sustainable*, it will be regenerative. You won't be slowing down harm. You'll be building systems that actively restore ecosystems, empower communities, and reimagine economies. AI will help you identify patterns, repurpose resources, and track long-term outcomes that humans alone may miss.

And your teammates? They'll be in Seoul, Stockholm, or São Paulo—no big deal. AI-powered collaboration will have turned async teamwork into an art form. With real-time translation, automated workflows, and intelligent task matching, you'll work seamlessly across time zones without missing a beat.

> "We've never met in person. But my team spans four countries. Our AI assistant handles updates while I sleep. It's weirdly smooth."
> **—Mila, 24, startup founder**

The work world will have finally caught up to how you already think and collaborate—globally, flexibly, and with purpose at the center.

 # Your edge: Trace the tech that shaped you

Look back to step forward

You've already lived through tech shifts. Let's unpack what you've learned, how to build on it, and what these shifts have developed within you that you can take into your Workverse.

Step 1: Trace your tech shifts

Let's reflect on the changes you've already navigated, and what they've made possible. Think back on your school life, side hustles, or part-time jobs. What are three specific technology shifts you've lived through, and what opportunities did they create for you?

Reflection 1: Technology shift →

Write down what changed for you (e.g., Discord launched).

_____

_____

_____

_____

Reflection 2: What opportunities opened up? →

Note what that shift made possible (e.g., I got first access to new products and creator partnerships).

_____

_____

_____

_____

(Repeat this set three times for three different shifts.)

Step 2: Spot the strengths you built

Looking back on those moments, what new skills or abilities did you develop? Maybe it was commercial awareness, online negotiation, content performance tracking, or managing tricky feedback loops. Write them all down: you've already built more than you think.

_____

_____

_____

_____

Step 3: Discover what drives you

You've already built skills from every tech shift you've lived through. Now it's time to see what's really fueling them.

 If you started exploring Marlee back in Chapter 1, this is where you can go deeper. Log in at Marlee.com, click on your avatar (top right), and open *My Profile & Results* to see your top ten motivations laid out clearly. Think of it as your motivation map: the exact drivers that explain why some things give you energy and others drain you.

Here's what you might spot:

- If you see *Tools* in your top ten, you might be energized by digital platforms and experimenting with apps.

- If you see *Problems*, think about the kinds of content, games, or ideas you're drawn to: is it about fixing things or reimagining them?

- If you see *Systems*, maybe you naturally build workflows for your study, job apps, or group projects.

_____

_____

_____

_____

_____

Once you know these, you can start to find a through line: the patterns already shaping how you learn, work, and create.

> "You've already done the hard part in experimenting. The key is to now find out what makes you thrive."
> —**Coach Marlee**

Take the lead: You've got the edge, now use it

Every shift you've experienced has made you stronger. Every experiment—even the ones that bombed—helped you figure out what works (and what definitely doesn't).

The tools are changing. Fast. But so are the possibilities. You don't need to predict the future. You just need to know how to step into it with curiosity, creativity, and confidence. Every tech shift is a stepping stone and opportunity, if you're looking for one.

Up next: We're diving into what happens beyond traditional work, and how Gen Z is reshaping what work means. Because in the Workverse of 2035, your job title might not exist yet, but your impact? That starts now.

CHAPTER 3

Redefining Career and Workverse: 2035 Starts with You!

TL;DR

Why Gen Z isn't climbing "the ladder", you're building your Workverse.

By 2035, work will be fluid, project-based, global, and purpose-led. You won't chase promotions: you'll curate your growth.

- **You'll design your own work life:** shaped by energy, purpose, and flexibility.
- **Reinvention is your new rhythm:** curiosity and learning agility matter most.
- **Human skills are your edge:** especially critical thinking, ethics, and big-picture insight.
- **AI is a collaborator, not a threat:** your judgment and creativity lead.
- **Impact beats job titles:** you'll be hired for what you deliver, not where you sit.

Why the future of work isn't a career ladder, it's a work life you curate

Forget job titles. Forget climbing a corporate ladder. By 2035, the very structure of work will be unrecognizable compared to the models earlier generations relied on.

The model of one employer, one path, one profession? That script has already been retired. And in its place, a new Workverse is emerging, one that's modular, flexible, and radically personal. A place where your work life is shaped not by hierarchy or tenure, but by how you choose to learn, collaborate, experiment, and contribute.

In this chapter, we're talking about you and the new shape of work that's forming around you. This is about the shift from career paths to work lives you design. From outdated definitions of success to purpose-driven projects. From climbing someone else's ladder to building your own Workverse.

This isn't about mastering tools. It's about mastering the way you want to live and work, on your terms.

Let's explore eight bold visions that are already changing what work can be, so you can start shaping your own path with clarity, intention, and confidence.

But first: What even was a traditional career?

Let's take a moment to rewind. What even was a "career path"? For earlier generations, work followed a relatively predictable trajectory: education, employment, promotion, and retirement. Between 2020 and

2023, that formula started to shift. Remote and hybrid work models shattered location barriers and traditional hierarchies. And from 2023 onward, generative AI triggered a new wave of disruption, replacing repetitive tasks, expanding what's possible, and changing how teams are formed, managed, and rewarded.

By 2035, the days of staying with one employer for decades will be rare. Baby Boomers often spent 10 to 15 years—or even an entire career—with the same company. Gen X has averaged five to ten years per role, while Millennials typically change jobs every three to five years. Gen Z, the most mobile generation yet, is already switching roles every one to three years, seeking flexibility, growth, and alignment with personal values.[9] The rules have changed, and they're still changing. This chapter unpacks why that shift is the future.

From career ladders to designing your own work life

The old-school idea of climbing a single, fixed career ladder? That era is quietly dissolving. What's replacing it is something more flexible, more creative, and way more personal. It's your own evolving Workverse. Instead of fitting into a system designed decades ago, you now have the opportunity to shape your work life around your energy, your values, and your idea of success.

For Gen Z, this shift changes everything. You're not stuck in roles that don't fit or waiting years for someone to say you've "earned" the next rung. You're curating your own path: one that might include a mix of part-time work, freelance projects, startups, learning cycles, activism, side hustles, or creative gigs.

Today, about 40% of Gen Z workers are earning money from *both* a full-time role and a side hustle.[10] The world is moving toward a project-based economy powered by purpose, not position, and you're entering it right as it's taking off.

> "The future is not something we enter. The future is something we create."
> —Leonard Sweet, American futurist and cultural theologian

This shift is being driven by a few big forces. Automation is making many traditional roles redundant. AI and gig platforms like Upwork, Fiverr, Uber, and DoorDash are giving individuals more control. And culturally, Gen Z is rejecting outdated definitions of success: ones that center around status, job titles, or working long hours for approval. You're likely choosing something else: freedom, well-being, learning, and impact.

And that's the opportunity here. This is your chance to work on what matters to you, not just what pays the bills. You can build a work life that flexes with your personal seasons: exploring, pausing, pivoting, and experimenting as you grow. But designing your own Workverse takes clarity and self-awareness. With no clear roadmap, you'll need rituals to check in with your direction and define success on your own terms, not someone else's.

A few strategies can help. You might start by creating a personal operating system using Notion or Tana to track your projects, learning, and energy shifts. Marlee can support you in building a *Workverse Map* that reveals your motivations, strengths, and evolving work themes, so you can keep your self-awareness current as you grow and change. (You'll dive deeper into your *Workverse Map* in Chapter 15.)

Use platforms such as LinkedIn, Behance, Dribble, or Contra to showcase your multi-project identity. And don't forget to schedule quarterly check-ins with yourself to ask: *What's working? What's changed? What do I want next?* You're not chasing a promotion; you're curating a life.

> "We all have two choices: we can make a living or we can design a life."
> —Jim Rohn, business philosopher

Reinvent. Reskill. Redefine what's possible

The idea of a skill set you evolve to master over a ten-year period, like your parents or leaders and managers did? It's being replaced by something far more dynamic: lifelong reinvention. You'll reskill, pivot, and evolve many, many times throughout your work life, and that's a strength, not a setback. Curiosity and adaptability are your real long-term advantages.

> "The future of work is learning-more specifically, the future of work is learning faster than the competition."
> —Heather McGowan, future-of-work strategist

For Gen Z, this might feel natural. You might already value curiosity, creativity, and freedom to change. But reinvention is now the norm. Industries are changing fast. New tools and roles are emerging constantly. Some of the most important jobs in 2035 don't exist yet. What's going to keep you energized and relevant isn't static expertise; it's your willingness to reflect, shift, and explore what's next.

This shift is driven by rapid changes in tech, climate, health, and global systems. As work becomes more modular and AI automates routine tasks, the value of a static skillset declines. What rises in value? Flexibility, learning agility, and your ability to realign your work with your evolving interests and motivations.

The upside? You're never stuck. You're not locked into one identity, one path, or one definition of success. Reinvention gives you momentum. It allows you to move forward with confidence, even when everything around you changes.

To navigate this well, pay attention to what motivates and energizes you, not just what's trending, and build your own learning rhythm. Use Marlee's *Over Time Board* to track how your motivations shift. Design a "Skill Stack Map" so you can see what's growing, what's fading, and where you're curious. Journal regularly; capture your evolving identity, not just achievements. Each quarter, run a mini reinvention cycle: pause, reflect, realign, and explore.

And as your identity and skillset evolve, so will the qualities that set you apart. In a world full of automation, your most powerful edge is the part of you that can't be replicated.

"When the going gets tough, the tough reinvent."
—RuPaul, drag performer, singer, actor, personality, and author

And that's the mindset to carry forward: one of constant, empowered evolution.

Human skills are your superpower in an AI world

As the Workverse evolves, it's easy to assume that technical skills will take over everything. After all, AI can write reports, design solutions, and even produce art. But when you step back, the real future of work becomes clear: human skills aren't becoming less important, they're becoming the most valuable currency of all.

As we've seen, the value of uniquely human capabilities continues to grow exponentially. These three capabilities in particular will determine your success in a tech-saturated world: critical thinking, big-picture thinking, and ethics. These are the essential traits for navigating a world where machines can perform tasks but can't make the bigger judgment calls that shape progress.

Critical thinking means holding two opposing ideas in mind at the same time and stepping back to explore them from different angles. In a world flooded with AI-generated options, your ability to stay curious, question assumptions, and resist black-and-white thinking will set you apart.

> "The real advantage humans have is the ability to rise above the activity and challenge what's being presented to us."
> —Dan Negroni

Building on that, big-picture thinking gives you the ability to connect the dots: to rise above the endless list of tasks and hold onto the purpose behind them. AI can complete assignments, but it can't ask whether we're aiming at the right goals. Big-picture thinkers will be the ones setting direction, not just following it.

> "I realized I was getting buried in to-dos and missing the bigger picture. So I made one small change: I started journaling weekly to reflect. Now I ask better questions in meetings, and my manager noticed the difference."
> —Liam, 24, product manager

And most importantly, ethics will serve as the invisible framework that holds the future together. As technology accelerates, it will be up to humans, not machines, to decide what kind of society we want to build. Machines can optimize for speed or efficiency, but they can't choose to prioritize fairness, sustainability, or dignity.

> "Values are lived, not programmed, and it's up to each human, and indeed, each generation, to carry them forward."
> —Michelle Duval

And while critical thinking, ethics, and big-picture insight form the foundation of your future value, they're just the beginning. What really brings these human skills to life—what makes them felt across teams and projects—is how you show up in relationship with others. In a world run by algorithms, it's your empathy, emotional intelligence, and ability to connect that turn good ideas into meaningful change.

> "Encode Justice captures the sense that our organization's goal is not about stopping all technology, nor is it about putting an end to innovation. Instead, we are trying to re-imagine what we do have and build justice into the frameworks of these systems from the very beginning."
> —Sneha Revanur, "The Greta Thunberg of AI"

While automation reshapes industries, companies are realizing that it's *human-first skills* that hold teams and strategies together. Soft skills—which we prefer to call *human skills*—are becoming hard currency. AI may help generate ideas or automate tasks, but it's your cross-cultural communication, emotional intelligence, empathy, and decision-making that truly create impact.

This is your opportunity to lead from a place of strength. Gen Z already values purpose, authenticity, and community: these traits are exactly what the future of leadership and collaboration will require and can help shape a whole new evolution or even revolution at work.

Use Marlee's visualized Boards to identify where your natural collaboration, decision-making, or empathy shines brightest. It's tempting to let AI think for you, but the more you outsource your judgment, the less you grow as a leader. Stay grounded in what only *you* can bring.

Try building team rituals that foster empathy, such as retros, story-sharing, or emotional check-ins. Join spaces that stretch your communication style, such as cross-generation or cross-functional teams.

Learn how to tell stories that move people, not just present data. The edge you'll need isn't technical, it's human. And like any muscle, it gets stronger with use.

> "The future of AI is not about replacing humans, it's about augmenting human capabilities."
> —Sundar Pichai, CEO of Google

We've talked about the human skills that will make you invaluable in the AI era: critical thinking, big-picture thinking, and ethics. But what if those skills are just the beginning? What if the real shift ahead isn't just about preserving your humanity, but unlocking more of it than we've ever accessed before?

The human potential revolution

As AI picks up speed and takes more off your plate, something unexpected is beginning to unfold, not in the machines, but in us. While algorithms handle the routine, the future of work is becoming more human than ever.

> "The future of work won't be defined by how fast we think, but by how deeply we connect. As AI expands the mind's capacity, our next frontier is human presence: intuition, emotional resonance, and consciousness will become the real skills of the century."
> **—Michelle Duval**

Over the next decade, you'll see breakthroughs that stretch the boundaries of what's possible. Researchers are already developing brain-to-brain communication technology—early forms of telepathy made real through research.[11] Neural implants are letting people control devices just by thinking, unlocking new dimensions of human influence over the world around us.[12]

Futurists even suggest that teleportation of information, expanded human senses, and untapped intuitive abilities could become part of our lived experience by 2035.[13]

For Gen Z, this opens a new kind of growth. This is about stepping into abilities we haven't even fully imagined yet. As AI takes on more of the mechanical work, humans will be free and challenged to discover new depths of creativity, connection, and consciousness. The future of work is becoming deeper and more powerful.

The opportunity? You get to explore what it really means to grow, not just in skill, but in awareness. The challenge is learning to slow down enough to notice it. In a fast-moving Workverse, staying grounded, intuitive, and intentional will be just as critical as staying productive.

Start tracking your inner shifts, not just your outputs. If you want to thrive in this next era, tune in: not only to the world around you, but to the one within. As technology moves faster, your edge will come from going deeper.

> "As AI begins to outpace what we know, the real edge will belong to those who trust themselves. In a world full of noise, people will follow leaders who know who they are, what they stand for, and how to create value for others."
> —Dan Negroni

AI teammates will free you to focus on what matters

In the future Workverse, AI will be a teammate. It won't replace human insight; it will amplify it. The real shift is learning how to direct the machine, not just use it. One analysis suggests that up to 30% of all working hours could be automated by 2030, rising to about 45% by 2035 in advanced economies.[14] You'll co-create, strategize, and build alongside systems that help you move faster, test more ideas, and reduce the heavy lift of repetitive tasks. The key is to stay in control of the story.

By 2027, 86% of organizations worldwide plan to embed big data or AI technologies into their operations,[2] a clear sign of things to come. In offices, AI assistants will draft emails, generate reports, and crunch data; in factories, smart robots (or "cobots") will collaborate with human workers on assembly lines; in customer service, chatbots will handle basic inquiries; and in healthcare, doctors will rely on AI for data analysis and diagnostic support. In short, nearly every professional is likely to have some form of AI teammate on their team by 2035.

> "I think that because of artificial intelligence, people will have more time to enjoy being human beings. I don't think we'll need a lot of jobs."
> —Jack Ma, Alibaba co-founder

With AI doing the heavy lifting behind the scenes, you can shift your focus toward the work that truly matters: problem-solving, creativity, and purpose-driven impact. That's the sweet spot: where you're leading with vision while your AI teammate handles the admin, the data, or the first draft.

This shift is already happening with generative technology, personalized assistants, and custom workflows. The magic isn't in the tools themselves; it's in how you use them. You decide when to delegate, when to override, and when to step in with your judgment.

> "Human-only work is our future. Anything that cannot be digitized or automated will become extremely valuable."
> —Gerd Leonhard, futurist and author

And as your collaboration with AI becomes second nature, the way work itself is structured continues to shift too. AI can help you ideate faster, test more ideas, and bring your work to life with less friction to focus on impact and purpose-led work.

Start experimenting. Use platforms like Canva, ChatGPT, Midjourney, and Notion AI to ideate and execute faster. Create an AI playbook that shows you how to ideate, outline, research, or brainstorm in ways that work for your mind. Journal weekly to track where AI helped, and where you added the most human value.

As AI evolves, your greatest advantage will be staying grounded in what makes you *you*. The more automation accelerates, the more your values, judgment, and personal impact will matter. This is your invitation to stay curious and reflective, to make sure the work still feels like yours.

> "Tech can supercharge your impact, but it's your sense of purpose that keeps it on track. We're discovering that integrating AI with clear personal values develops solutions that truly improve people's lives."
> **—Michelle Duval**

Ask yourself regularly: *What would I do without AI here?* Keep tuning in: *Is this aligned with what I care about? Am I bringing something only I can offer?* Deeply invest in understanding your unique contribution through technology such as Marlee, journaling, or coaching, and use that insight to create impact in the world. That's how you ensure your contribution stays human, authentic, and deeply meaningful.

And as work becomes more project-based, the walls around where and when that work happens are dissolving too.

Unleash impact through task-based work

By 2035, you'll be hired for outcomes, not titles. The rise of gig platforms, automation, and remote teams has made traditional job descriptions feel increasingly outdated. What companies need now is agility: people who can jump in, adapt quickly, and get sh*t done.

In the Workverse, it's your impact that counts, not the seat you hold. You'll be brought into projects to contribute, collaborate, and deliver. Work will be shaped around missions and tasks, and your ability to produce results will matter far more than what's listed on your résumé.

"I hardly ever hear *Who's in charge?* anymore. It's always, *What problem are we solving, and who has the best skills for it?*"
—Andre, 31, UX Designer

The best part? You don't have to wait years for a promotion to prove your value. You can start making an impact and getting recognized for it, fast.

This kind of work moves quickly. It favors people who are adaptable, self-aware, and motivated by meaning. One day, you might be designing a campaign with one team, the next, researching trends for another. Each mission builds your track record. Every deliverable becomes a chance to earn trust, grow your reputation, and show how you solve real-world problems.

The challenge? Task-based work can feel isolating or fragmented if you're not intentional. When you're moving between projects, you'll need to create your own rhythm, structure, and sense of belonging.

Energy, visibility, and connection won't just happen; you'll need to design systems for them, especially across projects.

The right strategies can make a big difference. Use platforms like Notion, Trello, or Airtable to plan, reflect, and showcase your work. Build a project portfolio that highlights what you've delivered, not just where you've worked. Use Marlee to align your tasks with your natural energy and motivation patterns. Create a weekly reflection ritual by asking: *What problems did I solve? What impact did I have?*

And just as importantly, make space for real connection. Whether online or in person, prioritizing your relationships helps you stay emotionally grounded and avoid the loneliness that can come with independent or remote work. You'll need to be intentional about this.

While the way we measure work is changing—less about roles, more about outcomes—when and where we work is shifting just as radically. Gen Z is entering a Workverse unbound by location, time zones, or even a single employer. That's where we head next.

The rise of borderless, flexible work

Where and when you work is becoming increasingly fluid. Offices are optional. Time zones are flexible. Companies are tapping into global talent clouds, while new platforms make it easier to collaborate across borders and work asynchronously. Entire teams are now operating across continents, in real time, in the cloud, or not at the same time at all. Even futurists like Reid Hoffman predict that the traditional nine-to-five workday will be "*extinct*" within the next decade.[15]

That kind of freedom can be incredible, especially for a generation that values autonomy and purpose. Research already shows that Gen Z prioritizes meaningful work and flexibility over loyalty to a single company, and the future is leaning hard into that preference.[16]

You'll have more control over designing your work life around your energy, your needs, and your lifestyle. Want to take a midday hike or work from your hometown library? That's no longer a dream scenario; it's becoming the norm.

But freedom comes with responsibility. Without built-in boundaries or watercooler conversations, you'll need habits to stay visible, connected, and motivated when no one's looking over your shoulder.

> "My first freelance project was terrifying. No one cared what hours I worked; they only wanted results. But after a few wins, I realized . . . this freedom comes with trust. You earn it by being clear and delivering well."
> —Malek, 24, freelance data analyst

Start by crafting a portable "work identity": a standout digital presence and project archive that travels with you, like your LinkedIn profile or personal portfolio. Use async communications such as Slack, Notion, and Loom to collaborate across time zones, and schedule regular "offline" resets to avoid burnout in always-on environments.

Understand your unique motivational patterns using Marlee to find the right mix of in-person and remote interaction that keeps you energized. And don't underestimate the power of rituals—virtual coffees, weekly co-working check-ins, team story sessions—to build real connection across the distance.

> "Hybrid work doesn't happen by chance.
> You need to be intentional, proactive, and thoughtful
> to make it work properly."
> —Miroslav Miroslavov, CEO of OfficeRnD

Thrive in a multigenerational team

One of the most defining parts of your future work life won't be the tech; it'll be the people. Specifically, the *range* of people. As more individuals work longer, delaying retirement due to economic shifts and evolving work identities, it's likely that by 2035, you'll be collaborating across five generations at once.

The future of work won't just revolve around AI and automation; it will also demand that you thrive within complex human dynamics across generations.

You might be working alongside Gen Alpha creatives, Gen X leaders, and Baby Boomer decision-makers: all with different communication styles, values, and expectations around work. From Slack etiquette to how feedback is delivered, succeeding in this environment will take empathy, adaptability, and a sharp eye for decoding generational signals.

Rather than treating those differences as friction, treat them as your edge. You'll have access to decades of wisdom, strategy, and experience while bringing your own digital fluency, fresh thinking, and energy to the table.

Gen Z has a rare opportunity to lead as generational translators, bridge-builders, and inclusive collaborators earlier than any cohort before. Learn how to adapt, build trust, and speak each group's language, and you'll stand out fast.

Without self-awareness and the right strategies, though, these dynamics can quickly become challenging. You might misread someone's intent, spark conflict, or feel dismissed. Don't assume someone's resistant to change; get curious about what they need to feel confident. You'll often be the one flexing first, but doing so intentionally can build enormous influence and trust (we'll explore these risks further in Chapter 5).

Use Marlee's *Generational Boards* to explore where your motivations align or diverge from your teammates. *Ask Marlee* for real-time coaching on how to connect or persuade someone from a different generation. Try reverse mentoring: trade tech insights for leadership wisdom.

Build your *Convincer* strategy with Marlee to uncover what others need to be persuaded: some rely on data, others on stories, others on consistency over time. And practice inclusive communication by blending Gen Z's text-based style with earlier generations' preference for face-to-face or visual feedback.

In a future powered by both humans and machines, your ability to lead across generations will be essential.

This generational power shift is a permanent shift in how work gets done. And it's giving Gen Z a unique opportunity to step forward, reshape the rules, and lead with a different kind of influence. But to do that, you need a foundation of human skills that set you apart.

Now build your human skills map

You've just explored eight future-of-work visions, but every one of them relies on human skills. Whether it's self-management, collaboration, adaptability, or influence, these skills are your edge in an AI-driven Workverse. That's why Marlee created the *Human Skills (Soft Skills)* Board, it helps you visualize your human strengths—and spot your growth edges—so you can keep building the most future-ready version of you.

Step 1: Spot your unique human skill

Your edge starts with one skill: the one that could unlock the biggest growth for you right now. Which of these three feels most relevant to strengthen?

- **Critical thinking**
  Think about the last time you were faced with two very different points of view. Did you feel pressure to choose a side, or were you able to step back, stay curious, and explore and critique both sides objectively?

- **Big-picture thinking**
  When you're deep in a task or project, how easy is it for you to zoom out and ask: *Why are we doing this? Where is this leading?* Do you stay connected to the bigger goal, or get pulled into the details?

- **Ethics**
  Picture a time you faced a tough decision at work or school. What guided you? What did you use as your moral or ethical compass? How clear are you on the principles you want to work and live by?

Circle the one that feels most important for your growth right now.

Step 2: Create your *Human Skills* Board

 Seeing your human skills visualized brings them into focus. Log in at Marlee.com, click *Boards* in the navigation, then under *Templates*, create your *Human Skills (Soft Skills)* Board.

Explore your personal insights in these charts:

- Emotional Intelligence (EQ)
- Problem and Risk Aversion
- Pioneering New Things
- Holding Others Accountable
- Critical Thinking

Hit *Generate Insight* and take a look:

- Which of your motivations are within the ideal zone
- Where do you have an opportunity to grow

Your Board reveals the human skills you already have, and the ones you can intentionally level up.

Note where there's room to grow

_____

_____

_____

Step 3: Set your development goal

Pick one human skill to focus on: it's easier to build momentum when you focus and strengthen one area at a time.

Here's how you can start developing it with Marlee's free coaching programs:

- **To develop critical thinking and your big-picture thinking** → go to *Coaching* and start the *Big Picture Thinker* program and *Reflection & Patience*.

- **To further develop awareness of your ethical guiding principles and values** → go to *Coaching* and start *Goal Catcher*.

Building your future starts with developing yourself.

List the programs you're keen to start

_____

_____

_____

> "You don't need to master all three today. But by getting curious about the one that matters most to you right now, you'll start developing the skills to enable you to thrive. I'll guide you step-by-step."
> —Coach Marlee

Where you go from here: Curate your next move

You've just explored what work could look like in 2035 and how your human skills will shape that future.

The Workverse isn't a place where you wait to be picked. It's where you choose your path, one task at a time. You need to learn what energizes you and lean into it.

In the next chapter, we'll explore the most promising industries emerging from this evolution. From climate innovation to performance optimization, you'll learn how to identify the opportunities that fit your values and fuel your growth.

Up next: Let's find the spaces where you belong and where your skills can truly shine.

CHAPTER 4

Gen Z's Opportunity: Your Next Step and Roles You'll Create

TL;DR

Why the most exciting roles of the future are yours to create.

From your next subject choice to roles in climate tech and neurotech still to be invented, the most exciting opportunities are shaped by your energy, values, and curiosity.

- **You'll shape the future by solving real-world problems:** not by filling outdated job titles.
- **Regenerative, immersive, and human-enhancing roles are rising fast:** Gen Z is already leading them.
- **Your motivations align with high-impact fields:** climate innovation, neurotech, and creator economies.
- **Micro-credentials and projects will matter more than degrees:** real-world proof of impact will win.
- **Your next role may not exist yet:** the clues are in what sparks your energy today.

Discover your next steps now, and the roles only you can invent ahead

What if your next job doesn't exist yet? What if you're not preparing for a path, but designing one? The most exciting work ahead is likely to grow out of emerging technologies, urgent global needs, and your own instinct to build something better. This chapter is your launchpad into roles that are rising fast, and others that haven't been named yet. From climate innovation to human-AI collaboration, this is where Gen Z's energy, values, and curiosity can lead the way.

You don't need to have it all figured out. You just need curiosity, energy, and the courage to keep asking a better question: *What kind of impact do I want to have, and where do I come alive doing it?*

Across the next few pages, we'll spotlight some of the most exciting fields shaping our world, from climate tech to neurotechnology, from the Metaverse to human performance optimization. In each one, you'll get a quick snapshot of:

- What's happening in the industry and why it matters
- Why Gen Z is uniquely positioned to thrive in it
- The pathways and skills that can help you step in, or even break new ground

Whether you see your future self as a climate technology strategist, a brain-computer interface designer, or something no one's named yet, you'll find inspiration here. Not to lock yourself into a job title. But to help you spot patterns, energizing themes, and real possibilities.

Your work life won't follow a single track. It will be shaped by the roles you say yes to, the ones you outgrow, and the ones you imagine from scratch. This chapter is your springboard.

Finding your next step in the Workverse

Before we leap into 2035, let's ground in your very next steps, the choices in front of you right now.

Start with what energizes you

Before you worry about what's "hot" in the job market, ask yourself a simpler question: *What energizes me most?* The best choices for subjects, degrees, or first jobs come when they align with your motivation, not just market demand. Even the fastest-growing industry won't feel like a fit if it drains you every day. Your motivations are your compass; use them to guide the next step.

Scan the horizon, close to home

It's easy to feel lost in global headlines about AI taking jobs or climate change reshaping industries. Instead of doomscrolling, check the sources that actually matter for where you live. These reports may not be binge-worthy, but they're like the spoiler alerts for which industries are about to boom (or fizzle out).

Globally, the World Economic Forum's *Future of Jobs Report* reveals rising and declining industries. In the US, Georgetown's jobs outlook maps future career paths. In the UK, government labor reports spotlight which sectors are hiring. In Australia, the *Jobs and Skills Report* highlights the qualifications employers are seeking. In your own country, search "[your country] jobs outlook + [insert current year]"—most governments publish one. Think of it like scanning the map before picking your route.

Match your studies to signals in the market

Choosing your school subjects, college or university courses, or training pathways isn't about guessing the "perfect" role. It's about matching what excites you with where opportunities are growing. If reports show health, tech, and green industries hiring, and you feel energized by science or systems thinking, that's your signal. If they show creative digital economies expanding, and you're lit up by design or storytelling, that's another signal. Don't chase trends blindly; notice the overlaps between your energy and market demand.

Think in horizons, not forever plans

No one expects you to lock in a forever plan, nor should you. And the Workverse doesn't even work like that anymore. Try thinking in horizons instead. Here are some examples of how you might think about your next steps. But remember: in today's fast-moving Workverse, things will likely shift faster than this. Treat these as example horizons, not fixed timelines.

- **Now → Next two years:** Focus on building transferable skills (communication, digital literacy, collaboration). If you're still in school, that might mean subject choices. If you're already working, it could mean projects, side gigs, or short courses that stretch you.

- **Next three to five years:** Explore internships, certifications, career experiments, or early jobs that test your fit in rising industries. If you've already started your career, this could look like volunteering for cross-team projects, trying a new role, or even making a lateral move to learn faster.

- **Beyond five years:** Stay flexible. Roles will evolve, and so will you. The goal isn't to lock in one forever path, but to keep momentum and choice alive.

Even if you change direction later (and you likely will, multiple times), you'll still be building skills that travel with you, no matter whether you're 16 and planning subjects, 22 finishing a degree, or 27 making your first big work pivot.

Use the tools around you

You don't have to figure this out alone. Most governments have free labor market data portals you can search. LinkedIn job trends show you which skills are appearing in job posts right now. Marlee's *Individual Results* and *Future Roles Boards* help you track what energizes you and match it to future roles. Don't underestimate the power of a conversation. Reach out to someone two or three steps ahead of you, and ask what surprised them about their path. Often, the best insights come from those just a little further along.

All of these tools are here to give you signals, but the real power comes in how you connect them back to yourself.

Now, let's explore what's opening up and what's calling you forward. As you explore the fields ahead, notice how they align with what naturally energizes you. That's why the roles in this chapter are paired with Gen Z's core motivations; to help you see not just what's possible, but why you personally may thrive in it.

Why these roles? A match for Gen Z's motivations

You're not looking for just any job; you're looking for work that energizes you, fits your rhythm, and aligns with what matters most. That's exactly how this chapter was designed.

The roles you'll explore in the next few pages weren't chosen at random. They're based on findings from *The Gen Z at Work Study*, the largest global study into what motivates Gen Z at work. The data shows clear patterns: Gen Z is likely to be drawn to structured, purpose-driven work where precision and real-world impact collide.

Each section ahead pairs future-facing roles with motivational traits that Gen Z tends to find energizing as a starting point for discovery.

We'll delve deeper into these motivations in Chapter 6, and in Chapter 7, you'll personalize them based on your own unique interests and passions. But for now, this chapter is your window into where your generation's strengths could thrive in the Workverse ahead.

Climate tech: Designing a regenerative future

Work is shifting from static roles to dynamic missions, and climate tech is one of the clearest examples.

Two in ten Gen Zs and Millennials have already changed jobs or industries to better align their work with their environmental values, with another quarter planning to do so in the future.[17] According to *The Gen Z at Work Study*, Gen Z is especially motivated by problem-solving and systems thinking. It's a powerful combination, and it positions Gen Z to help lead this transformation.

The climate solutions of 2035 won't stop at sustainability. Already today, climate roles are among the fastest-growing jobs worldwide—from renewable energy to environmental data analysis. If you're studying science, engineering, or policy now, you're stepping into one of the strongest growth fields of the next decade. But the climate solutions of the future will go further, toward full regeneration. Regenerating ecosystems, reimagining cities, and redesigning entire industries will be at the core of this next wave. And climate tech will power it all.

Regeneration means building systems that restore what's been lost. From algae-powered buildings to AI-coordinated rewilding efforts, the projects emerging now are bold, systemic, and deeply collaborative.

For 86% of Gen Z, a deep commitment to purpose-led work is important.[17] Whether it's engineering living materials that purify air and water, designing circular economy systems, or using AI to map climate risk and resilience, the work ahead is layered, mission-led, and transformative.

> "I have learned you are never too small to make a difference."
> —**Greta Thunberg**

We're already seeing Gen Z take the lead.

"I co-created a platform that tracks composting initiatives across my region. I never expected it to be picked up by local government, but now I lead a team expanding it."
—**Taylor, 23, founder and community lead**

The climate economy is gaining momentum, and it will be shaped by the next generation of thinkers, builders, and creators.

"By 2035, regenerative technologies will be a pillar of every business function, and the next wave of workers will lead the charge in climate-positive solutions."
—Dan Negroni

Let's explore some of the most exciting roles emerging in this space. At the end of Chapter 4, you'll find a detailed breakdown for each one, including the impact you'll drive, the Gen Z advantage, and the skills and pathways to help you design a meaningful work life.

- **Ocean Restoration Engineer:** Design technologies that heal marine ecosystems, from coral regeneration to ocean deacidification. Build a work life where science meets hands-on impact.

- **Regenerative Climate Engineer:** Create climate tech that restores, not just sustains. Work with AI, bioengineering, and living systems to shape a thriving, resilient planet.

- **Planetary Data Wrangler:** Use satellite data, AI, and environmental modeling to decode Earth's signals and guide smarter climate decisions for researchers and changemakers.

Neurotechnology and bioengineering: Where tech will transform life

By 2035, breakthroughs at the intersection of biology and technology will reshape how we heal, grow, and enhance life itself. Neurotech startups are attracting record levels of funding, with experiments from wearable memory aids to lab-grown tissues already moving from labs to early markets.

> "I joined a uni research project 18 months ago just to get lab hours. Now I'm helping test brain-computer interfaces on stroke patients. It still blows my mind that something I scrolled past on Reddit is what I'm wiring up in the lab."
> —Sofia, 21, neuroscience student

From brain-computer interfaces that restore memory to lab-grown tissues that regenerate organs, this field is moving fast. The roles emerging here are precise, complex, and deeply collaborative, exactly the kind of environment where Gen Z tends to thrive.

According to *The Gen Z at Work Study*, your generation is energized by problem-solving, systems thinking, and reflective iteration. You're wired to test, verify, and improve, which makes you well-suited to fields where precision is essential. Neurotech and bioengineering depend on this kind of thinking, where structure supports creativity and outcomes are driven by evidence, not guesswork.

> "We are not limited by the technology we have. We are limited by the imagination we apply to it."
> —**Albert Einstein**

For Gen Z, this is a space to design with purpose and improve life at its most fundamental level.

Here's where your generation's precision and pattern recognition could truly transform human health and potential. Flip to the end of Chapter 4 for the full breakdown of each role: the impact, the Gen Z edge, and how to get started.

- **Cognitive Enhancement Engineer:** Build neurotech tools that boost learning, focus, and mental resilience. Where AI meets neuroscience, your work life fuels human intelligence.

- **Biofabrication Specialist:** Use tissue engineering and 3D bio-printing to grow organs, create smart prosthetics, and design biomaterials that heal people and the planet.

- **Neuroethical Policy Advisor:** Shape the future of brain-tech by building guardrails for AI-enhanced cognition. Blend ethics, law, and neuroscience to protect human rights.

Metaverse ecosystems and creator economies: Virtual experiences that will connect

The next generation of virtual worlds is already taking shape: expansive spaces where people will learn, heal, build businesses, and form communities beyond geographic borders. For Gen Z, who tends to move naturally across platforms, the Metaverse will feel less like an escape and more like an extension of everyday life. Right now, job growth in the Metaverse is being driven by demand for immersive experiences, from gaming and virtual concerts to digital marketplaces.

Your generation's strong affinity for exploring new tools, navigating interconnected digital ecosystems, and jumping into active creation will put you at the forefront of designing these experiences. According to *The Gen Z at Work Study*, you're likely to thrive in environments that reward rapid iteration, systems thinking, and creative autonomy.

Whether you're crafting hyper-realistic environments, developing interactive story worlds, or engineering new ways for brands and communities to connect, the future Workverse will be powered by creators who know how to bring technology and human connection together.

> "I started freelancing by designing digital sets for YouTubers. Now I run a collective that builds therapeutic VR environments for mental health orgs. I didn't follow one clear path, but each project moved me closer to work that aligns with my purpose."
> —Maria, 25, creative technologist

As virtual spaces become more sophisticated, the work will demand technical fluency and an intuitive understanding of how systems and communities evolve—all strengths Gen Z could bring to the table.

These virtual frontiers will need architects, strategists, and experience designers who understand both technology and human connection: areas where Gen Z already brings a natural edge. Head to the end of Chapter 4 for the full role breakdown: the impact you'll drive, the Gen Z advantage, and how to build your path forward.

- **Immersive Tech Curator:** Design AR, VR, and mixed-reality experiences that transform how people connect, learn, and engage. Your systems thinking becomes immersive storytelling.
- **Metaverse Architect:** Build virtual worlds that people can live, work, and play in, from social hubs to digital campuses. Where creative design meets connection, Gen Z leads the way.
- **Creator Economy Strategist:** Shape the next era of digital entrepreneurship. Design new ways for communities to earn, share, and grow value across immersive platforms and ecosystems.

"I wasn't sure how my gaming passion would fit into work. Now I'm helping design virtual wellness spaces for young people with anxiety. Turns out, creating virtual worlds is just another way to create change."
—Lucas, 23, Immersive Experience Designer

Amplifying human potential: Unleashing human performance optimization

As technology transforms what we do at work, the next frontier will focus on amplifying how we think, feel, and perform, not just automating tasks, but unlocking the vast, unexplored terrain of human potential. Wellness tech and performance platforms are already among the fastest-funded startups, showing just how much the world is investing in human potential.

> ☆ "I started tracking my sleep with a wearable just to fix my late-night study habits. Now half my friends are experimenting with apps and supplements to stay balanced at uni. It feels like we're all beta-testing the future of human performance."
> —**Jayden, 20, student-athlete**

The Gen Z at Work Study found Gen Z has a strong motivation for embracing diverse styles, strengths, and approaches, positioning your generation well to lead this revolution. With the highest preference for tolerance and inclusion compared to earlier generations, Gen Z is uniquely motivated to design systems that help every human to flourish, bringing science, technology, human energy, and insight together to enhance well-being and performance.

> "Helping people perform at their best starts with seeing them clearly, accepting their differences, understanding how they work, and showing them what they're capable of.
> That's the kind of leadership Gen Z is built for."
> —Dan Negroni

By 2035, wearable tech, AI-driven coaching, neuroenhancement strategies, and resilience science will redefine how teams are built and supported. Future roles could include designing personalized cognitive immersive experiences, creating biometric-based productivity platforms, or pioneering new approaches to leadership development for multigenerational teams.

Gen Z's tendency to value different perspectives, foster collaborative environments, and champion human growth will be one of the most sought-after superpowers in the Workverse ahead.

As we move from optimizing processes to optimizing people, these roles will define how humans reach their full potential in the age of augmentation. Flip to the end of Chapter 4 for the full breakdown of each role: the impact, the Gen Z edge, and how to build your future-fit skill stack.

- **Human Augmentation Specialist:** Engineer next-gen prosthetics, neural implants, and wearable tech that expand human capabilities. Where biotech meets performance, you'll lead the evolution.

- **AI-Powered Wellness Strategist:** Design hyper-personalized health tech that adapts in real time. Combine data, behavior science, and AI to help people live and perform at their best.

- **Neuro-Resilience Coach:** Use brain science and biofeedback to build focus, adaptability, and mental strength. In a world of overload, you'll help others stay clear and steady.

How to get ready for what's next

The common thread

Across every industry, the roles shaping 2035 have something powerful in common: they demand more than technical know-how. They demand human strengths: creative problem-solving, empathy, resilience, systems thinking, and a strong sense of purpose.

Across every sector, Gen Z's preference for building connections, embracing diverse perspectives, and guiding technology toward meaningful outcomes will define the next era of work. It's about shaping roles around the problems you want to solve, and the human spark you bring to them.

> "Where you see a critical issue—environmental, social, or technological—that's your invitation to innovate. Don't wait for permission."
> —**Michelle Duval**

If you're wondering how to start shaping your own path, we'll explore that shortly.

How Gen Z will learn in the future Workverse

In the future, traditional degrees will be just one piece of the puzzle, and not the most important one. What will set you apart is the work you've done, the problems you've solved, and the skills you can apply right now.

Micro-credentials, hands-on experience, and proof of impact will carry real weight. Employers won't be asking where you went to school; they'll be asking what you've created, contributed to, or changed.

> "I started learning product design through free platforms and micro-courses. Two years later, I've built a freelance UX career and mentored others in my community to do the same."
> —**Aarav, 22, self-taught UX designer**

In fact, by 2035, 80% of people worldwide believe newly acquired skills, like those gained from micro-credentials, will be just as valuable as traditional degrees.[18]

Whether it's earning a badge in climate storytelling or completing a five-week lab on brain-computer interfaces, your ability to learn quickly and apply knowledge in real time is what will set you apart.

 Discover the roles that light you up

Your Workverse, your way

Every generation asks, *Where do I fit?* But Gen Z tends to ask, *Where can I thrive?* Whether it's immersive design, regenerative tech, or optimizing human potential, your next opportunity starts with curiosity.

See which future roles match your motivations

 We've created Workverse *Future Roles* Boards in Marlee precisely for this, to help you map the future roles from this chapter against your own unique work style and motivations. Some of these roles may open up in the next few years, while others will emerge as new industries take shape over the coming five years and beyond.

As you work through the steps below, open your *Future Roles* Board and use the *Generate Insights* feature to take a look at how both near-term and future opportunities connect back to what truly energizes you.

Step 1: Consider what draws you in

Look back at the future roles and industries in this chapter. Which ones genuinely sparked your interest? Highlight or jot down three to five that lit you up.

Below each role, reflect on what draws your attention or attracts you to it. Then, jot down three to five points for each role.

_____
_____
_____

Step 2: Look for the hidden pattern

What themes connect the roles that energized you? Circle all that apply:

- Solving urgent real-world problems
- Creating immersive experiences
- Working with cutting-edge technology
- Optimizing human performance
- Building regenerative systems
- Something else?

_____
_____
_____

Then ask yourself When have I felt most engaged in similar activities before?

_____
_____
_____

Remember, if you're stuck, paste your list into your favorite AI tool and ask: "What do these roles have in common?" Sometimes a fresh lens reveals the theme you're missing.

Step 3: Explore what that says about you

Now that you've spotted patterns across the roles that sparked your energy, let's slow down and reflect on what those patterns reveal about *you*.

Are you drawn to work that makes a tangible impact? Do you feel energized by problem-solving, storytelling, or designing systems that help others thrive? These are clues about the values that drive your decisions, the environments where you feel most alive, and the kind of energy you bring to your team.

The goal of this step isn't to lock in your "forever job." It's to build clarity. When you understand what motivates you—what truly *lights you up*—you can start to align your gigs, courses, or collaborations around work that fuels your strengths.

_____

_____

_____

> "You don't need to know your whole path right now.
> But you can notice what energizes you.
> Start there, and I'll help you explore what's next."
> —**Coach Marlee**

Your future is taking shape. Now what?

Now that you've identified opportunities that light you up, let's prepare for the challenges you'll face in claiming them.

Up next: Explore the potential risks in this evolving Workverse and find out exactly how you can navigate them with confidence.

Future Roles

 ## Ocean Restoration Engineer

Impact and Mission	You'll be at the forefront of marine restoration, developing and implementing cutting-edge techniques like coral reef regeneration, kelp reforestation, and ocean deacidification. This role is all about designing and deploying technologies that restore damaged ecosystems and support biodiversity, ensuring healthier oceans for future generations.
Gen Z Advantage	Gen Z doesn't just want to learn about climate change; it wants to solve it. Many Gen Zers will feel energized by roles where you can get your hands dirty, experiment, and see the impact of your work firsthand. You'll be combining scientific knowledge, creativity, and hands-on problem-solving. If you love the idea of turning the ocean into your laboratory and blending science with regeneration, this path is for you.
Skills and Pathway	Start by building expertise in marine biology, environmental engineering, and ocean modeling. Get hands-on experience with habitat restoration technologies, AI-driven climate analysis, and underwater robotics to bring the future of ocean regeneration to life. Whether through research projects or internships, each step strengthens your impact and prepares you to lead.

 # Regenerative Climate Engineer

Impact and Mission	In this role, you'll design living systems that regenerate the planet, from bio-cities and atmospheric cleansing materials to AI-driven rewilding networks. You'll create nature-inspired solutions that restore biodiversity, replenish ecosystems, and build resilience, leading climate tech that doesn't just prevent damage but powers a thriving Earth.
Gen Z Advantage	Gen Z prefers steady, science-driven, high-impact environments where bioengineering, AI, and ecological systems work together to regenerate rather than merely sustain. With Gen Z's preference for problem-solving, you'll design planetary regeneration systems that make Earth healthier, more resilient, and more abundant than ever before. If you're drawn to climate tech, bioengineering, AI, and regenerative design, this is where you'll leave your mark.
Skills and Pathway	Build expertise in bioengineering, environmental science, and regenerative design. Explore AI-driven ecological modeling, planetary rewilding, and next-gen climate tech. Seek internships, research, or startup roles focused on living materials, restoration, and circular biodesign. In biotech, conservation, or climate infrastructure, each step strengthens your path to planetary renewal.

Planetary Data Wrangler

Impact and Mission	You'll be on the frontline of climate science and planetary monitoring, using AI, remote sensing, and satellite data to track climate shifts, biodiversity, and environmental patterns. Whether analyzing global reforestation trends or mapping ocean temperatures, your work ensures that scientists, policymakers, and conservationists have real-time insights to restore the planet.
Gen Z Advantage	Gen Z has a preference to think in patterns and connections, making your generation a natural fit for turning raw planetary data into real-world action. Gen Z may thrive in structured, problem-solving environments where AI, automation, and satellite tech fuel smarter climate solutions. The ability to track trends, translate data into impact, and communicate findings will help ensure that conservationists, researchers, and policymakers make informed decisions and regenerate the planet.
Skills and Pathway	Build expertise in data science, remote sensing, GIS mapping, and environmental modeling. Learn to analyze satellite imagery and use AI for ecological forecasting. Gain experience with Earth observation labs or climate tech startups to apply data in real-world renewal, and help shape a thriving, self-sustaining era of environmental intelligence.

 # Cognitive Enhancement Engineer

Impact and Mission	Breakthroughs in neuroscience and AI will shape human cognition. This role will develop neurotechnology to boost memory, learning, focus, and problem-solving through brain-stimulation wearables, AI-powered cognitive training programs, and biofeedback systems. Your work will help unlock cognitive potential, enhance mental resilience, and support recovery from neurological conditions. This is where technology will meet human potential and transform how we think and perform.
Gen Z Advantage	Gen Z has a preference for tools and technology, human performance, and ways to push limits and enhance abilities. Gen Z's curiosity for AI, neuroscience, and optimization tools may make your generation a natural fit for this role, where data-driven insights and real-world applications drive progress. If you're excited about neurostimulation, biofeedback, and AI-driven cognitive tools, this is your chance to shape the future of human intelligence.
Skills and Pathway	Develop expertise in neuroscience, AI cognition modeling, biofeedback systems, and neurotechnology while gaining experience with brainwave analytics, wearable tech, and performance optimization. Look for roles in neurotech startups, research labs, or biotech hubs where you can design tools that enhance how we think and learn.

Biofabrication Specialist

Impact and Mission	Imagine a future where lab-grown organs, bioengineered tissues, and sustainable biomaterials replace traditional manufacturing. As a Biofabrication Specialist, you'll be at the forefront of tissue engineering, regenerative medicine, and 3D bioprinting, developing breakthroughs that could eliminate organ shortages, revolutionize prosthetics, and create regenerative alternatives to plastics. Your work could mean printing functional human tissues for transplants, designing synthetic skin for burn victims, or developing biomaterials that self-repair and adapt to their environment.
Gen Z Advantage	Many Gen Zers will feel energized by applied science, hands-on innovation, and technology that creates real impact. While some breakthroughs may take years to fully develop, you'll see progress through each prototype, experiment, and research milestone. If you love the idea of engineering the future of medicine and environmental regeneration, this path could be for you.
Skills and Pathway	Build expertise in biomaterials science, tissue engineering, and 3D bioprinting while gaining experience with biomedical research, regenerative medicine, and bioengineering labs. Hands-on work in biotech startups, research fellowships, or medical innovation hubs will prepare you to bring biofabrication from the lab to real-world applications.

Neuroethical Policy Advisor

Impact and Mission	Neurotechnology will advance—think brain-computer interfaces, AI-driven cognition tools, and mind-enhancing therapies—so the need for ethical guidance and regulation will be more critical than ever. In this role, you'll bridge the gap between science, ethics, and policy, ensuring emerging neurotechnologies are developed responsibly, equitably, and with long-term human impact in mind. Whether advising governments on data privacy for brain-computer interfaces or helping companies navigate the ethics of AI-enhanced cognition, your work will shape the future of neuroscience and human rights.
Gen Z Advantage	Gen Z prefers analytical and justice-driven thinking, making this an ideal space to explore. Gen Z is motivated to question the status quo, think critically about new technologies, and seek purpose-driven work that protects people's rights and well-being. Blending research, policy, and ethical reasoning will help ensure neurotechnology enhances humanity, not exploits it.
Skills and Pathway	Start by developing expertise in neuroethics, bioethics, policy analysis, and data privacy. Gain hands-on experience through AI ethics research, biotech law, or advocacy. Your path will unite human dignity and technological progress.

Immersive Tech Curator

Impact and Mission	You'll be designing and orchestrating immersive virtual experiences that blend virtual reality (VR), augmented reality (AR), and mixed reality (XR) to create compelling storytelling, education, and brand engagement. Whether it's building interactive museum exhibits, designing virtual concerts, or enhancing remote collaboration through spatial computing, your work will shape how people experience the digital and physical worlds as one.
Gen Z Advantage	Gen Z is likely to feel energized by working within virtual experiences that draw people in and evoke strong emotions. Gen Z's preference for systems thinking means your generation may instinctively know how to blend storytelling, tech, and engagement to bring ideas to life in a way that resonates.
Skills and Pathway	Develop expertise in VR/AR development, spatial computing, interactive storytelling, and user experience (UX) design. Gain hands-on experience in immersive media labs, gaming studios, or creative tech startups where you can experiment, build, and refine the future of virtual engagement.

Metaverse Architect

Impact and Mission	As a Metaverse Architect, you'll be at the forefront of designing virtual environments, digital cities, and interactive 3D spaces. From decentralized digital real estate to immersive social hubs, you'll be responsible for creating seamless, engaging, and functional virtual worlds that people can live, work, and play in.
Gen Z Advantage	Gen Z is likely to instinctively understand how virtual spaces should feel. Gen Z doesn't just see 3D models; as a generation, you see how people will interact, move, and connect in a way that feels natural. If you love gaming, creative design, and virtual environments, you'll thrive in shaping the next evolution of virtual spaces.
Skills and Pathway	Develop expertise in 3D modeling, game engines (Unity/Unreal), blockchain integration, and UX for virtual spaces. Gain experience through virtual world design projects, Web3 startups, or interactive virtual communities to build the foundations of next-gen virtual spaces.

Creator Economy Strategist

Impact and Mission	In this role, you'll shape the next evolution of virtual economies, immersive social experiences, and decentralized creative platforms. As the creator economy shifts from influencer-driven models to AI-powered, user-owned ecosystems, you'll develop strategies that empower virtual creators, brands, and communities to thrive in autonomous, tokenized, and hyper-interactive environments. Whether optimizing monetization for immersive worlds, architecting blockchain-enabled creator marketplaces, or designing next-gen interactive content formats, your work will redefine how value is created and exchanged in the virtual age.
Gen Z Advantage	Gen Z understands virtual cultures, influencer dynamics, and the value of online communities better than any generation. With your generation's technology mindset, content fluency, and passion for exploring new platforms, Gen Z is likely to see opportunities where others see trends. The ability to think strategically about virtual communities, branding, and monetization models will make Gen Z an essential voice in the creator economy revolution.
Skills and Pathway	Start developing skills in monetization strategy, platform design, and tokenomics. Gain experience in Web3, AI content, or creator startups. Strategic, big-picture thinking will set you apart.

Human Augmentation Specialist

Impact and Mission	From bionic limbs to AI-driven brain implants, this role is about enhancing human capabilities beyond natural limits. Whether developing wearable exoskeletons for injury recovery, neurotech implants to boost cognition, or sensory-enhancing prosthetics, your work will push the boundaries of what the human body and mind can achieve. This is where bioengineering, neuroscience, and AI will meet human potential.
Gen Z Advantage	This opportunity sits at the intersection of technology and human potential, playing directly into Gen Z's motivations. The ability to blend problem-solving, biotech, and hands-on innovation will shape how we move, think, and perform beyond natural limits.
Skills and Pathway	Develop expertise in biomedical engineering, AI-enhanced prosthetics, human-machine interfaces, and neurotechnology. Gain hands-on experience through research labs, biotech startups, or exoskeleton development projects to pioneer the next evolution of human augmentation.

AI-Powered Wellness Strategist

Impact and Mission	Imagine a world where AI personalizes health, fitness, and mental well-being in real time. In this role, you'll develop AI-driven health platforms, biohacking tools, and predictive wellness apps that will help people optimize their physical and mental performance. From AI-powered nutrition guidance to biometric-driven mental health support, your work will bring hyper-personalized wellness to the masses.
Gen Z Advantage	This opportunity prioritizes health and wellness, optimized through the use of technology. Your generation is likely to thrive creating data-driven, hyper-personalized solutions that empower people to perform at their best.
Skills and Pathway	Develop expertise in AI-driven health analytics, bioinformatics, behavioral science, and digital therapeutics. Gain experience with AI wellness startups, personalized health tech platforms, or biohacking research to revolutionize how people manage their well-being.

Neuro-Resilience Coach

Impact and Mission	By 2035, to manage stress, burnout, and digital overload, resilience will become a superpower. As a Neuro-Resilience Coach, you'll use brain science, AI-driven biofeedback, and personalized coaching to help people optimize focus, emotional agility, and cognitive endurance. From neurostimulation techniques to AI-powered mindfulness training, you'll guide individuals toward peak mental performance and resilience in high-pressure environments.
Gen Z Advantage	Mental resilience is a superpower. Opportunities blend science, tech, and psychology to help people stay focused, perform under pressure, and optimize their mindset for success.
Skills and Pathway	Develop expertise in cognitive neuroscience, biofeedback training, neurostimulation, and AI-powered mental health coaching. Gain hands-on experience in human performance research, mental resilience labs, or AI-driven therapy platforms to help individuals build stronger, more adaptable minds.

CHAPTER 5

Navigating the Risks Ahead Your Way

TL;DR

How to turn future risks into your personal edge.

The Workverse is shifting fast. New risks like burnout, distraction, and disconnection are real, but they're also invitations. When you stay connected to what energizes you, reflect intentionally, and lead with clarity, the risks don't slow you down; they sharpen your direction.

- **No one's mapping your path:** the ladder's gone. Create your own evolving *Workverse Map* based on values, energy, and direction.
- **Mastery beats panic learning:** focus your growth on purpose-driven development, not endless upskilling.
- **Human edge matters:** AI is fast, but your judgment, energy, and connection are irreplaceable.
- **What happens next is up to you:** take your lead with purpose.

The hidden challenges of tomorrow's Workverse, and how to turn them into your advantage

You're not alone if the future of work feels like a mosaic: project-based gigs, part-time roles, side hustles, AI-powered workflows, team collabs that span time zones, and learning curves that never flatten. It's exciting, sure, but it also comes with new risks that earlier generations didn't have to face.

This chapter isn't about fear. It's about awareness. Like any great navigator, your job is to learn how to read the currents. These risks aren't red flags that should alarm you. They're markers that help you map a smarter, more resilient path through the Workverse.

So what kinds of risks are emerging in the 2035 Workverse? Here are eight hidden challenges that are shaping how Gen Z will need to think about success, energy, and identity at work. And more importantly, how you can design and flourish around them.

Not taking ownership of your work path in a mosaic Workverse

In the past, as we explored in Chapter 3, work looked like a ladder. Generations before you would climb rung by rung, intern to assistant, manager to director. There was security in that simplicity. But for your generation, that model has quietly shifted. The future of work is no longer a linear climb; it's a mosaic. An ecosystem of projects, platforms, skills, and collaborations that may never fit into a tidy "old-school" job title. This shift offers more freedom, but it also introduces a subtle risk: drifting without direction.

What makes this especially challenging is that the traditional scaffolding, the predictable timelines, formal mentorship, and fixed job pathways are not there anymore. That means you need to be intentional about where you're going and why. Without that internal compass, it's easy to move fast and still go nowhere. You might find yourself saying yes to every opportunity, burning out in the process, or stepping into leadership roles without the mindset, support, or strategy needed to truly lead.

This is a professional and personal risk. Because when your work life lacks clarity, it doesn't just affect your job. It can erode your confidence, relationships, and well-being. Ambition without direction can quietly wear you down.

So what do you do in a world where no one's handing you the map? You make one. And not just once, but as a living document that evolves with you. That means getting clear on your own definition of success, beyond titles or external approval. For some, it's about impact. For others, balance. For many, it's about learning something new each season. Your task is to tune in regularly. What's energizing you right now? What themes keep showing up in your work? Where are you growing, or stagnating?

Start treating your work life as a series of seasons: moments of growth, periods of rest, times to double down, and times to reinvent. There will be no single template for career success to measure from, but there will be a pattern. Those who stay connected to their values, energy, and direction tend to thrive, even when the path isn't clear.

To navigate this mosaic with more clarity and confidence, a few simple strategies can go a long way. In Chapter 15, you'll learn how to build your own *Workverse Map*: a personalized guide that captures your motivations, strengths, and evolving direction. A Notion-style dashboard (or any digital space) can help you track shifts in your energy, projects, and skills along the way. Peer coaching circles and mentor-matrix tools can expand your perspective, especially when your most valuable mentors aren't older, but walking the path alongside you. And Marlee's *Motivational Analysis* and *Human Skills (Soft Skills) Board* can help make your values visible, even as they evolve.

And don't underestimate the power of reflection. A quarterly ritual, a moment to pause, check your compass, and adjust course, can bring coherence to even the most nonlinear path.

Because no one's going to build your work path for you. But with the right rhythm, mindset, and systems, you can build one that's not just successful, but uniquely yours.

Once you've started shaping your own path, another challenge quickly emerges: how do you choose what to go deep on? In a world overflowing with opportunities, skills, and platforms, the risk is spreading yourself too thin.

The next risk isn't about having *no* direction, it's about having *too many*. Let's explore what happens when the pressure to constantly learn leaves you feeling like you're never quite "ready enough."

Jack-of-all-trades, master of none: Never achieving mastery

You've probably heard it a hundred times: the future belongs to those who adapt. Keep learning. Upskill. Pivot fast, or get left behind. And while there's truth in that, it comes with a hidden cost. As we've explored, nearly half of all skills used in today's roles will be disrupted[1] and the pace of change will only accelerate. When every trend feels urgent and every job post lists ten evolving skills, it's easy to fall into a loop of nonstop learning without ever landing deeply on what matters most.

For Gen Z, the risk isn't laziness or lack of ambition; it's burnout by way of over-preparation. You start stacking courses, chasing credentials, and bookmarking podcasts, always waiting to feel "ready enough." But without structure the learning loop becomes a treadmill. You're constantly moving, but not always growing.

This doesn't just create fatigue. It can quietly fracture your sense of self. When your identity is tied to constant learning, it's hard to feel grounded in what you already *know and can do*. You may feel like you're a jack-of-all-trades, but master of none. And in the process, you miss out on the confidence that experience and mastery bring: the quiet power of *I've got this*.

What's behind this is a Workverse built on speed, not depth. Industries shift fast. AI automates skills you just learned. Platforms change. So the instinct to keep learning is valid. But the strategy needs to shift, from panic learning to intentional rhythm.

Before you jump into your next course, ask yourself: *Am I learning, or am I developing?* Learning is about acquiring something new. It can feel exciting, especially when novelty gives you that quick hit of progress. But development is deeper. It's about applying what you've learned, refining it through practice, and evolving over time. It's where mastery lives, and where real satisfaction is built. Think of it like downloading apps you never open. Learning without applying is just storage, not progress.

Over the next 10 years, think long-term. Focus on meaningful development, not just adding skills, but integrating them into who you're becoming. Ask yourself: *What do I need to deepen right now, to grow,* to solve, or to contribute in a way that matters? This is the essence of intentional learning: grounding it in a purpose that matters to you.

One of the most powerful ways to stay intentional? Find your *through line*, a deeper purpose or theme that helps you sense-check decisions when everything feels like an opportunity. Your through line isn't just about a job title or skill set. It's the deeper mission behind your work life. Maybe it's building inclusive communities, solving complex problems, or creating things that help others grow.

When you know your through line, learning becomes more focused, and development becomes possible and meaningful. You're not chasing every skill. You're developing in a way that reflects who you are and what you care about.

> "Growth isn't about learning everything. It's about knowing your through line and choosing a next step that aligns."
> **—Michelle Duval**

That also means being intentional about *where* you learn. Seek out environments that genuinely support your growth. The most impactful workplaces don't just talk about development; they build systems, space, and cultures that make it real. Look for organizations that align learning with values, create room for experimentation, and empower you to shape your own direction.

Leading organizations are already showing what this can look like:

- **Google:** For years, Google has encouraged employees to explore ideas beyond their core role, especially when those ideas solve real-world problems. A powerful example came in the wake of September 11, when engineer Krishna Bharat built what became Google News to help people access a broader range of perspectives during a time of global crisis. What began as a personal need—to make sense of overwhelming, conflicting headlines—grew into a tool used by millions. This wasn't about chasing a trend; it was about responding to the moment with purpose. And that's what intentional learning often looks like: seeing a problem that matters, then growing the skills to do something about it.[19]

- **Canva:** It fosters a culture where employees are encouraged to pursue work that aligns with their strengths and passions.[20]

> "I began in the recruitment team at Canva, but my true passion has always been creating experiences and environments where people thrive. With this purpose in mind, I pitched a new role aligned with my strengths, and, after weeks of insightful chats with leadership, I transitioned into a people experience role-one of the most rewarding of my career."
> —Charlotte Anderson, Head of People Experience at Canva

- **Mercadona:** In Spain's supermarket world, where low wages and limited development are the norm, Mercadona flips the script. It pays well above minimum wage and actively invests in its people, with more than four million hours of training logged in one year alone. As repetitive tasks get automated, Mercadona doesn't cut corners; it creates space for more meaningful, engaging roles and promotes from within. And it's not just about work. Through its Legacy Project, the company backs local communities with food donations, disaster relief, and support for grassroots initiatives. At Mercadona, development is deeply embedded in the culture.[21]

These examples illustrate a broader shift toward purposeful learning, where growth is guided by intention, not just learning for learning's sake. But this isn't just something companies can do. It's something *you* can put into practice, starting with how you track your own development.

Create a "Skill Stack" Board that shows what you've mastered: tools, human skills, experiences, and outcomes. You're building something, not collecting badges. Seeing it mapped out will help you find your through line and remind you that you're developing.

Not every gap needs to be filled. Know when to go deep, when to pause, and when to say, "Not right now." That boundary is a form of wisdom, not limitation. You're not defined by what you haven't learned; you're shaped by how you grow with intention, focus, and courage.

Strategic learning beats reactive learning. Use microlearning stacks to organize what you want to learn in the next 90 days. Marlee's *Over Time* Board can help you see how your human skills and motivations evolve with time. Each quarter, take time to reflect: What are you learning, and why? What's energizing you, and what's no longer serving you?

And don't try to do it all alone. Join peer learning groups or communities where knowledge flows both ways, and growth is supported together. Purposeful development doesn't have to be a solo journey; it's strengthened when you're learning alongside others who are asking similar questions.

Give yourself permission to pace it. You don't need to jump into every course or trend. It's okay to say, *I'm enough with what I've learned, for now. My next step is to apply, not acquire.* That's not falling behind, it's growing with intention. Because mastery isn't about knowing everything. It's about knowing what matters now and trusting yourself to grow from there.

But learning isn't the only muscle that needs attention. In a world where AI tools are everywhere and answers are instant, there's another risk quietly building: losing your ability to think deeply, critically, and for yourself. Let's explore what happens when convenience starts to erode your judgment, and how to stay sharp in an age of automation.

Losing judgment in the age of AI

There's no doubt about it; AI is becoming your most powerful teammate. It writes, designs, codes, analyzes, and learns at a speed no human can match. According to research, nearly two-thirds of organizations are now implementing AI at scale,[22] and many workers are beginning to question where they fit in. But as this technology transforms how work gets done, a quieter risk is emerging: losing touch with your own judgment.

This is about remembering what makes you irreplaceable. Judgment, intuition, ethics, and contextual awareness are the things that can't be templated or automated. These are the skills that will matter most in the next chapter of work. If you begin to hand those over to machines without noticing, you risk becoming a passive executor. Someone who presses buttons but doesn't shape outcomes.

What's driving this threat is convenience. AI is fast, helpful, and often impressively accurate. But when you get too used to asking ChatGPT to make every decision or summarize every article, you start skipping the slow work of critical thinking. You stop weighing trade-offs. You accept output without asking: *Is this true? Is it right? Is it what I believe?*

Over time, this can blur the line between speed and wisdom. You may find yourself delivering polished work that's missing some things that are vital: original insight, emotional depth, or ethical clarity. At work. In relationships. In life.

So here's what you need to remember over the next 10 years: AI is your tool, not your guide. It's here to support your thinking, not replace it. The most fulfilled and future-ready people won't just know how to use AI, they'll know when to pause it. They'll be the ones who protect space for reflection, practice curiosity, and lean into work that asks more from them than fast answers.

> "When ChatGPT started helping me draft copy, I was like: *Do I even matter here?* But then I noticed the best-performing content still came from stuff I'd lived through: my voice, my take."
> —Keenan, 24, content strategist

Conscious co-creation is the new baseline. It means checking yourself before you hit send. It means asking: *Where did I lean too hard on the algorithm? What context might it be missing?* It means layering AI output with your own research, values, and lived experience. It also means nurturing the slow skills—lateral thinking, ethical reasoning, complexity, tolerance—because those are the muscles that will matter when decisions carry real consequences.

There are strategies that can help you stay sharp. Reflection prompts built into your AI workflows can nudge you to ask better questions. Decision-making frameworks can help you weigh not just efficiency, but ethics and impact. Tools like Feedly or Glasp let you go deeper into nuanced, human-written thought rather than defaulting to summaries. And one of the most underrated habits? Practicing simple Socratic routines.

A Socratic routine is just a fancy way of saying: *ask better questions—out loud or in your head—until you uncover deeper thinking*. It's based on how the philosopher Socrates guided his students, not by giving answers, but by helping them discover their own. In your work life, it might sound like:

- *What assumption am I making here?*
- *Is there another perspective I haven't considered?*
- *What would make the opposite true?*
- *Why do I believe this is the right decision?*

Think of it like mental debugging. You're sharpening your judgment. In a world full of instant answers, the best thinkers are the ones who pause and ask the next question.

And don't skip the team reflection moments. Regular debriefs that ask *What did we miss, and why?* Keep judgment alive in group settings too. Because thinking critically is easier when it's modeled, expected, and practiced together.

AI isn't here to take your place. It's here to test your discernment. In a future where anyone can generate content, insight will be the real currency. And judgment, the human kind, will be what sets you apart.

And as you strengthen your judgment, remember this: human consciousness is still largely unmapped. You're part of a generation that will begin to uncover dimensions of awareness we haven't fully explored, expanded senses, intuitive capabilities, even new forms of connection and creativity that feel more felt than taught. As AI handles the known, your real potential may lie in the unknown: those deeper layers of insight, perception, and presence that technology can't replicate.

But accessing those deeper states, your intuition, your presence, your creative potential, requires more than just intention. It requires energy. And in today's fast-moving Workverse, that energy is constantly under pressure. When everything speeds up—your tools, your timelines, your expectations—it becomes harder to slow down, recover, and reconnect with what matters. — — — — — —→

So as we move forward, let's talk about what happens when that pressure builds. When the pace doesn't ease up. When you're always on. Because the next risk isn't about your ideas, it's about your well-being.

Burnout from an always-on Workverse

The Workverse is faster than ever. Every platform you use—Slack, Notion, LinkedIn, even the calendar on your phone—reinforces one message: *keep going*. Stay productive. Stay visible. Stay learning. But that constant motion is taking a toll. In 2024, 91% of people said they experienced high pressure or stress at some point, and one in three felt that way "often" or "always." Gen Z is being hit hardest: nearly half of 18–24-year-olds reported stress from overtime, cost-of-living pressure, and feeling isolated at work.[23]

When work becomes constant, it quietly becomes unsustainable. You keep pushing: learning new skills, saying yes to side projects, filling your calendar with more. Until suddenly, there's no space left to breathe. The result isn't mastery. It's burnout. And often, it doesn't look like a breakdown; it may feel like numbness. Low energy. Fuzzy thinking. A creeping sense that no matter how much you do, it's never quite enough.[24]

What researchers now understand is that burnout isn't just about doing too much; it's about doing too much of what doesn't match your internal drivers. One study found that when your work doesn't align with your underlying motivations, it creates what psychologists call "motivational incongruence." Over time, that mismatch quietly erodes your cognitive clarity and emotional engagement. Your brain gets foggy. Your energy dips. Even success starts to feel hollow. Burnout, in this sense, is the biological cost of misalignment.[25]

Gen Z is entering the workforce at a time when that misalignment is easier than ever to fall into. You're navigating a Workverse shaped by performance metrics, digital visibility, and constant comparison, where output is often rewarded more than alignment. And without space to reflect, it becomes easy to drift away from what actually energizes you. Over time, the line between effort and identity starts to blur.

So, how do you navigate this over the next 10 years without losing yourself? First, by rejecting the idea that "more" is always the goal. Start setting enough goals: targets that define a healthy threshold, not just an impossible ceiling. Progress is valuable, but it needs space to breathe. Success is about what you can sustain. A big part of that is aligning your motivation with how you manage your energy, a strategy we'll explore more deeply in Chapter 12.

The solution isn't to push harder. It's learning to work in a way that works for you. That starts with noticing what brings you back to life; we call these your recovery rituals. Maybe it's sketching, dancing, hiking, venting with a friend, or just staring out a window without your phone. These can be your fuel.[26]

The next shift? Strategic pauses. Tiny ones. A walk around the block. A breath between meetings. Even two minutes with your eyes closed. These moments help you reset before the pressure spills over. Ask yourself: *What's draining me? What's still meaningful? What do I need more, or less, of right now?*

And here's a reframe that changes everything: Start budgeting your energy, not just your time. Think of your energy like currency. Where do you spend too much? Where do you recharge? Map it out. Then build your week around that rhythm so your work doesn't just get done, it gets done with you intact.

You'll also need to audit your inputs. In a world saturated with content, growth can become shallow if you're always consuming and never integrating. Not every podcast, article, or course moves you forward.

Sometimes, growth isn't about adding more but letting go. *Unlearning* outdated habits, unrealistic expectations, or borrowed goals creates space for clarity. It's how you stop doing what drains you, and start building a rhythm that sustains you.

There are strategies that can support this new rhythm. Digital minimalism planners help reduce noise. Input fasts—temporary breaks from content or stimulation—can help you reset. Marlee's *Motivation Analysis* visualizes where your natural drive is strongest, and where you might be forcing energy into areas that don't align. Burnout check-ins and well-being dashboards turn vague stress into visible data. And rest planning templates—yes, you can *plan* for rest—help make recovery a part of your strategy, not a sign of weakness.

Even small rituals can shift your default. Try a monthly "unlearning" session: *What belief, habit, or goal no longer serves me? What boundary needs reinforcing? And what deserves celebration, even if it's simply choosing to rest?*

You don't need to earn your pause. In fact, your future depends on it. Because in the always-on Workverse, those who thrive won't be the ones who never stop. They'll be the ones who know when to stop, why it matters, and how to start again with clarity, not just speed.

But there's another kind of burnout that doesn't always come from doing too much; it comes from feeling emotionally alone while doing it. When your days are full, but your connections feel empty. That's the next risk: disconnection in a hyper-connected world.

Loneliness in a digitally focused world

Work has become more flexible, global, and connected, on the surface. Yet, beneath the flurry of notifications and video calls, a more fragile reality is unfolding: many are quietly working alone. For Gen Z, this carries a significant emotional cost.

Reports show that 29% of Gen Z feels lonely, more than double the rate of Baby Boomers and the Silent Generation at 14%.[27] Despite this, most interventions still focus on the elderly, highlighting a gap in addressing the needs of younger generations in workplace cultures.

As task-based work spreads and in-person moments shrink, the rituals that once tethered us to teams, mentors, and shared purpose are dissolving. There are fewer hallway chats, fewer personal check-ins, and fewer organic ways to feel seen. When that happens, loneliness starts to seep in: not just as a feeling, but as a silent drain on creativity, motivation, and mental health.

> "Sometimes I finish a whole day of remote work and realize I haven't spoken to a single person. I miss the casual stuff: the side chats, the office weirdness. Not just the work."
> —Aria, 23, marketing coordinator

This isn't just about missing people; it's about missing meaning. Connection at work is the emotional infrastructure that helps you stay engaged, take risks, and feel like what you're doing matters. Without it, even high-performing workers can feel invisible. Your ideas may be noticed, but your presence isn't felt. And that disconnect can lead to disengagement, burnout, or a sense of "why bother?"

What's driving this shift is the unbundling of work from place. We now live in a Workverse where you can finish a whole project without speaking to anyone out loud. Where collaboration happens in silent tools, and validation comes through emoji reactions. This isn't inherently bad, but it means more of the responsibility to build a connection now falls on *you*.

That's the shift to embrace over the next 10 years: connection is no longer built in; it's self-authored. And that's a skill. One that calls for conscious rituals, digital fluency, and emotional visibility.

Start by designing your own connection rhythms. Think about what helps you feel grounded and seen, whether it's a weekly peer check-in, a "Life Wins" channel with your team, or a regular voice note swap with a friend who gets the pressure you're under. Prioritize live connection when you can, but don't underestimate async rituals either: those moments of acknowledgment and presence matter, even on delay.

> "Our team has this Slack channel where we drop non-work stuff, like music we're into or random life updates. It sounds small, but it's often the only place I feel like my teammates are actual people, not just profile pictures. When I switched teams and didn't have that, I felt completely disconnected within weeks." -------
> —Jamie, 26, UX designer at a fintech startup

You'll also need to become fluent in both digital and human signals. What does a tired emoji really mean? When someone stops showing up on Slack, what might they be navigating? Strengthen your relational radar by tuning into tone, silence, and subtle cues. This is how you build psychological safety and trust in teams where physical presence isn't guaranteed.

> "Belonging won't be handed to you in the future of work; you'll need to cultivate it, protect it, and create it for others. That's how real connection begins."
> —Dan Negroni

Tools can help, but only if you use them with intention. Try journaling apps or voice memos to process your day when no one's around. Use Marlee's 1 to Many Team Board to explore what motivates your teammates emotionally, not just what they produce. Set up check-in templates that ask *How are you really?* not just *What's the status?* And curate your support ecosystem like it's part of your job, because for your well-being, it is.

In a digitized world, loneliness will be addressed with more authenticity. That means showing up authentically with your values, your boundaries, and your emotions, and giving others permission to do the same.

You don't always need to be surrounded to feel connected. But you do need to be intentional about how you create, protect, and grow your community, even across a screen.

While connection supports your emotional well-being, your financial foundation is what allows you to grow, take risks, and rest when you need to. The next risk centers on what happens if that safety net is missing.

Financial stress if you're not building a safety net

For earlier generations, work often came with built-in safety nets of steady paychecks, employer benefits, and a clear sense of what a "good job" meant financially. But that world has changed. Today, Gen Z is entering a financial landscape shaped by a whole new structure of work.

Employers are now leaning into "talent clouds," deploying high-skill gig workers across AI, cybersecurity, and product roles as a cost-saving alternative to full-time hiring.[28] This shift offers flexibility for companies, but for Gen Z, it increases the risk of job instability, inconsistent income, and a lack of traditional benefits. It's a structural shift and it's redefining what financial security looks like in the Workverse: less about guarantees, more about self-built resilience.

In this reality, the biggest financial risk is going unprepared. The deeper threat? Living in constant low-grade financial stress that can be quiet, exhausting, and always in the background. When you don't have a financial buffer, you're more likely to say yes out of fear than out of clarity. You may undercharge, overwork, or take roles that drain you, just to keep afloat. Over time, that erodes not just your bank account, but your energy, confidence, and ability to grow on your terms.

What's driving this shift is bigger than you. Global economies are more volatile. The gig and creator economy is booming. And traditional job benefits are disappearing, replaced by DIY systems that require you to build your own safety net.[29] These changes offer flexibility, yes, but without strong support systems, they also put more pressure on *you* to build a sense of security that used to be built in.

That's why the next 10 years will ask you to think differently about money, not just as survival, but as strategy. This is about building financial systems that give you breathing room. It's about creating a "buffer mindset", a foundation that helps you say yes to aligned opportunities and no to ones that drain you.

Start by understanding what drives your financial decisions. Is it stability? Freedom? Impact? Lifestyle? Knowing this can help shape the income strategies that work best for you. Then, begin diversifying, small at first. A freelance skill here. A digital product there. A savings ritual you can stick to. These are the building blocks of your financial foundation.

> "I made more freelancing last month than I did in my old retail job, but I also had no idea how much would come in this month. It's like winning and panicking at the same time."
> —Mateo, 25, video editor

Charge for the *value* you create, not just the hours you work. That mindset shift alone can change your trajectory. And remember that money moves in cycles, so plan for sprints and rest. There will be seasons where you go all in, and others where you reset. What matters is that you don't build your financial plan around constant output.

Tools can make all of this easier. Budgeting platforms like YNAB are designed for variable incomes, not just a salaried life. Shared insurance models and buffer-fund rituals offer a safety net beyond traditional benefits. Creator pricing calculators help you price your work fairly in a fast-moving economy. And online communities such as financial coaching groups or peer-led pricing forums can help you stay aligned with your worth, even when imposter syndrome creeps in.

What if policy shifted to support your buffer mindset?

As you build your own financial buffer with freelance gigs, savings rituals, or community support, there's another possibility on the horizon, a systemic shift that could change the way income works altogether.

Universal Basic Income (UBI) is no longer a fringe idea. Cities like Barcelona have already piloted it. In one program, called B-*Mincome*, residents received a monthly stipend that allowed them to cover essentials, no strings attached. That stability gave people room to create, contribute, and collaborate. One recipient, Sora, 25, used her stipend to build an interactive platform that teaches kids about nutrition and mental health. Without the weight of rent stress, she partnered with local schools and nonprofits to launch her idea, and early data showed it outperformed most after-school programs in student engagement.

UBI has its critics. It's not a perfect model, and it's not a replacement for all the strategies you're building today. But it's a signal. As traditional employment structures fade and gig work becomes the norm, more governments are beginning to explore how to reduce financial fragility through public policy, including gig-worker protections, portable benefits, and income subsidies tied to environmental or caregiving contributions.

> "If you're someone who dreams of building something meaningful but worries about the risk, this is your reminder: systems are shifting. Your shot to shape change might come sooner than you think."
> —Dan Negroni

This is your invitation not just to prepare, but to participate. Financial empowerment isn't only about what you build, it's also about what you *advocate for*. The more Gen Z voices shape these future systems, the more likely they'll reflect your values of fairness, flexibility, and freedom.

Money doesn't have to be a source of shame, anxiety, or survival stress. It can be a tool for spaciousness, stability, and self-determination. But only if you treat it that way proactively, reflectively, and with the same care you give to every other part of your well-being.

And once you've built that foundation, the next challenge isn't just personal, it's interpersonal. Because even with your finances in check, your work life doesn't happen in a vacuum. The next risk is all about navigating the team dynamics that emerge when five generations work side by side.

Conflict at work from not embracing the incredible value of a multigenerational Workverse

Picture today's workplace as a rich living tapestry woven from different generations, perspectives, and ways of working. In today's environment, it's common to find up to five generations collaborating side by side.[30] Each generation brings a wonderful confluence of perspectives to contribute and positively impact the Workverse. But that mix of energy and experience can easily lead to tension, especially when communication styles clash or unspoken biases creep in. For Gen Z, you might find your fresh perspectives dismissed or struggle to influence decision-making across generational divides.

This is about missed growth opportunities. When generational disconnects aren't addressed, misunderstandings can create friction, stall innovation, and limit the mutual exchange of ideas that drive a thriving workplace. The very differences that could be your greatest asset turn into obstacles, holding back not just your professional growth but also the collective potential of your team.

At the heart of this challenge is a clash between history and evolving expectations. Earlier generations may lean on hierarchy and experience-driven intuition. Gen Z often brings data, agility, and a desire for collaboration.

Without shared language or mutual understanding, these differences can turn into missed connections, misread feedback, and growing frustration. But with awareness, they become fuel for shared influence where co-leadership replaces control, and learning flows both ways, title or no title.

So, how can you bridge this generational divide over the next ten years? The key is to become a translator and a connector within the work environment. Start by learning to spot the different communication styles around you and what they're really trying to say. This is about developing a "translation toolkit" that helps you bridge values, share feedback, and harness influence effectively. It's about building small, inclusive micro-communities within larger teams where every voice, no matter the age, feels heard and finds resonance.

Consider embracing co-leadership as a model of collaboration rather than a battle for dominance. When you partner with colleagues who bring different generational strengths to the table, you unlock a powerful blend of data and storytelling, intuition and experience. Look for ways to cultivate reverse mentoring partnerships where insights flow both ways, and every conversation becomes an opportunity to learn.

> "Jonas built his success through handshakes and in-person deals. I design pitches with AI and interactive media. At first, we were in totally different worlds. But in a reverse mentorship, I showed him how immersive content could elevate his game, and he showed me how trust and presence can close million-dollar deals. We both walked away sharper."
> —**Carla, 25, designer**

Marlee was designed to help you navigate this exact challenge. Marlee's *Generational* Boards visually map the core values and motivators of each generation. You can compare your own motivational preferences with broader trends using Boards such as *Gen Z and Me* or *Baby Boomers and Me*, which highlight your biggest points of alignment and potential friction.

Each Board allows you to explore how your work style compares across generations, and you can click *Generate Insights* to help shape more thoughtful connections, feedback, and collaboration.

Inside each Board, you'll also find visualized motivational data that shows how different generations prefer to make decisions, communicate, and build trust at work, helping you tailor your approach in cross-generational teams.

In the grand tapestry of a multigenerational work environment, the key is not to erase differences but to honor and integrate them. By mastering cross-generational communication, building inclusive cultures, and leveraging targeted tools, you can turn a potential source of conflict into a wellspring of creativity and mutual empowerment.

But collaboration is only part of the story. Because once you're expected to lead, without strong modeling or real feedback loops, the next risk appears: finding yourself stuck in an echo chamber, leading without alignment, support, or intention.

The echo chamber without strong leadership around you

There was a time when leadership came with built-in structure: formal programs, long apprenticeships, seasoned mentors who helped you navigate conflict, pressure, and decision-making. That system? It's dissolving. In today's flatter, faster-paced organizations, traditional management layers are thinning, and coaching moments are harder to come by. Technology has accelerated this shift. So has the pressure to do more with less. As a result, many young workers are stepping into leadership moments without the modeling or guidance that earlier generations had.[31]

For Gen Z, that means you're often asked to lead before you've seen leadership in action. You're expected to guide projects, manage diverse personalities, and make decisions, all while wondering if you're doing it right. Without feedback loops or clear examples to draw from, leadership becomes reactive instead of intentional.

> "Everyone looked to me for decisions because I understood the project best, but I had zero training on how to actually lead people. I was constantly second-guessing whether I was being too directive or not directive enough. It took months to realize I was already leading, just without the recognition or support."
> —Zoe, 24, project lead

Zoe's not alone. Many Gen Z leaders are figuring things out in real time, with no safety net. And that lack of support can feel like an echo chamber. You're moving fast, solving problems, and making progress, but without feedback, pushback, or real guidance, it's hard to grow past your current level.

Over time, this can leave you directionless. Visible, but unsure how to evolve. And it's not personal. It's structural. As workplaces flatten and remote work becomes more common, organic guidance and mentorship, and in-the-moment modeling have become rarer. The pressure to figure it all out alone is rising.

Leadership today is about how you show up, how you build trust, and how you influence without needing a spotlight. You don't need permission to lead, but you do need intention. And over the next 10 years, one of the most valuable skills you can build is your leadership range: knowing when to collaborate, when to step up, when to step back, and how to calibrate your influence to the moment.

> "The next era of work will belong to the emotionally intelligent, those who know how to build trust, navigate conflict, and bring people together even when everything else is changing."
> —**Michelle Duval**

Start by building your own leadership mentors. Find a few people who won't just cheer you on, but they'll call you forward. Peers. Collaborators. Mentors who challenge your assumptions. These people help you practice leadership with both vision and accountability.

Then, look for your leadership moments. They often hide in plain sight: giving thoughtful feedback, aligning your team during a moment of confusion, or authentically speaking up when clarity is needed. Leadership lives in the micro-moments, not just the milestones.

And feedback? Don't wait for it. Ask for it, early, often, and with intention. Treat it like your compass. Because if no one's reflecting back what they see, you're just building habits in a vacuum.

Tools can help you stay grounded, but only if they're tied to how *you* work best. Start with Marlee's *Human Skills (Soft Skills)* Board. It helps you spot the motivational traits behind your influence style, so you can lead in ways that feel natural. Sprint templates give you space to reflect: *Where did you step up this week? Where did you hold back?* That awareness builds over time.

A decision journal is your space to track how you think, not just what you choose. The more you revisit your choices, the sharper your instincts become. And if you've never done a role model audit? Try it. That means stepping back to reflect on who you've been quietly influenced by, and whether they truly reflect the kind of person or leader you want to become. It's a powerful way to shift your focus from who you've been around to who you actually want to grow into.

If you're not getting the coaching you need, create it. Start a weekly check-in with a peer or mentor. Ask *What's one thing I did well this week? What's one thing I could try differently?* These small rituals build your confidence, insight, and trust over time.

Start Coach Marlee's program: *Personal Power* to give yourself permission to lead. You don't have to wait for someone to hand you a leadership title or enroll you in a development program. What matters most is knowing what matters to you, staying honest with yourself, and surrounding yourself with people who help you grow. That's your starting point. Everything else? You'll build it on the job, moment by moment.

But leadership only works when it's sustainable. Without the right systems, energy, and self-awareness, even the most driven leaders burn out. That's why building resilience is strategic. Let's step back and map your risk landscape so you can lead, grow, and thrive without losing your footing.

Build your resilience toolkit

Before we move on, take a breath. Risks don't look the same for everyone; what feels overwhelming for one person might fuel another. This is your chance to notice how the risks ahead show up for you and start building a toolkit that turns them into your personal edge.

Turn risks into advantages

Every risk we've explored—navigating uncertainty, self-leading in flat teams, burnout, or managing information overload—carries two sides: the challenge and the opportunity. This toolkit helps you pinpoint the risks most relevant to you and shape practical strategies that turn those challenges into your edge.

Step 1: Map your risk landscape

Look back at the workplace risks we've covered. Which three feel most relevant for you right now, or most likely to show up in your next chapter? Note them down, and rate how much impact you think each one could have (1 = huge impact, 5 = low impact).

Workplace risk	Impact (1-5)	Why this matters to me
Jack-of-all-trades, master of none: Never achieving mastery	4	I'm studying UX design, but I worry tools will automate parts of my future role

Step 2: Identify your current strategies

Chances are, you're already doing things to stay resilient, maybe without even noticing. For each risk you wrote down, ask *What am I already doing that helps me manage this?* It could be joining online communities to stay current, keeping a financial buffer, or leaning on mentors when things get uncertain. These small, existing habits are your resilience foundations.

_____

_____

_____

_____

Step 3: Discover your resilience patterns

Now head to your Marlee *Individual Results* Board. Your motivations can reveal where you naturally find strength in tough times. Look for the patterns; they're your built-in resilience strategies.

- If **External Reference** ranks high, your power lies in building strong networks for support and feedback during uncertain times.
- If **Problem-Solving** appears, you likely excel at spotting and addressing issues before they become crises.
- If **Breadth** is prominent, you may navigate complexity by seeing patterns and connections others miss.
- If **Procedures** ranks high, creating structured routines will be your anchor during rapid change.

_____

_____

_____

_____

Step 4: Design your personal resilience plan

Pick one risk that feels most pressing right now. Then, link it back to your motivations. What's one small, practical step you could take in the next 30 days to strengthen your resilience here?

For example:

- **If concerned about leadership gaps and have a high *External Reference*:** Schedule coffee with two senior colleagues to hear their leadership journeys and spot potential mentors.

- **If worried about digital isolation, with strong *People* motivation:** Start a weekly virtual coffee with teammates: no work talk allowed.

- **If anxious about skill obsolescence with a high *Systems* focus:** Map my current skills against three emerging industry trends to set my next learning priorities.

"Resilience is about stepping back to reflect and understand your strengths and how to apply them to the challenges you face in any given moment. The future belongs to those who can transform challenges into launching pads for growth."
—Coach Marlee

Own the risks, design your path

You've now explored eight of the most pressing risks shaping Gen Z's future in the Workverse. These don't need to become hurdles: they're invitations to step back, reflect, and design your work life from a place of awareness. With every risk you name and embrace, you unlock a path forward. That's the power of conscious work-life design.

As you travel to 2035, you need a clear sense of what matters and a rhythm that helps you stay in motion. You're not here to avoid risk. You're here to meet it with gentle kindness, clarity, confidence, and a toolkit that grows with you.

The most effective approach isn't resistance but adaptation and understanding how to leverage new realities while cultivating your irreplaceable human perspective.

So as you navigate the challenges we've explored in this chapter, remember this: The greatest risk isn't that you'll be replaced or left behind, it's that you'll underestimate your own adaptive capacity. Your ability to learn, unlearn, connect, create meaning, and bring your full humanity to work is your ultimate competitive advantage. The future belongs to those who embrace change while staying grounded in who they are. That future is waiting for you to shape it.

Now that you understand the landscape ahead, it's time to get specific about where you fit in it. Because thriving in this future isn't just about adapting to change; it's about aligning your work with who you are at your core.

Up Next: We'll discover your unique work sweet spot: the intersection where your natural motivations meet marketplace demand.

Part 2
Finding Your Place in the Workverse

Forget following a path designed for a workplace that no longer exists. This is your backstage pass to designing a work life that fits you. In this part, we'll help you map your motivations, uncover your edge, and start building something in the Workverse that feels unmistakably yours.

CHAPTER 6

The Gen Z Superpower Sweet Spot

TL;DR

Why your generation's strengths are exactly what the future needs.

Gen Z isn't just adapting to change; you're creating what's next.

- **You're built for collaboration:** you lead through co-creation, not control.
- **You learn fast and act faster:** your hands-on approach to tech gives you a practical edge.
- **Purpose fuels your choices**: you seek impact, not just paychecks.
- **You thrive in async, digital-first environments**: clarity and autonomy matter more than airtime.
- **You solve real problems with precision**: your detail-oriented mindset is in demand.
- **You create change that lasts:** reflection and patience give you space to solve problems deeply.

Discover the motivational strengths that give your generation an edge

So far, we've looked outward, tracking the biggest forces reshaping work, from AI to flexible models to the rise of new industries. But now, the spotlight shifts inward. Because building a work life that energizes you doesn't start with roles or trending skills, it starts with knowing how *you* work best.

This chapter marks the start of Part 2, and the heart of this playbook. From here on, we draw directly from The Gen Z at Work Study, Marlee's original research with more than 81,000 Gen Z individuals across 159 countries. You've seen this study mentioned earlier, but now, we're going deeper. These findings are about you: your motivations, your natural strengths, and how your generation is already reshaping the Workverse from the inside out.

What if the secret to thriving at work is about tapping into the way you're wired to contribute?

> "The future workplace doesn't need you to change who you are; it needs you to fully embrace your generation's unique strengths."
> **—Michelle Duval**

This chapter is your mirror. Let's explore the motivational superpowers that set your generation apart, and how you can use them to design a work life that fits *you*.

The superpowers that make Gen Z stand out

What gives your generation a real edge isn't just that you're digital natives or driven by purpose; it's how you approach work from the inside out. Let's explore Gen Z's motivational strengths and how they're already reshaping what great work looks like.

Collaboration comes first: Your co-leadership edge

The Gen Z at Work Study found that Gen Z is more likely than any earlier generation to seek feedback, share decision-making, and work collaboratively. You're not driven by ego or old-school "top-down" authority; you're energized by co-creating solutions with others.

This plays out in your preference for structured teamwork and shared responsibility. You're naturally drawn to environments where ideas are shaped together, not handed down. And while earlier generations may mistake that for needing too much input, it's a strength. Cross-functional teaming, agility, and collaboration are now among the most in-demand skills across industries. In fact, the World Economic Forum lists collaboration and agility among the top five most critical skills for the future workplace.

You don't need to make every decision solo. You prefer to align, anticipate, and build consensus to avoid wasting time down the track. That's not slow, it's very often strategic. You're the teammate who keeps big projects moving without excluding others.

Fast tech adapters, hands-on learners

You're not just fluent in tech, you *think* in systems and tools. According to *The Gen Z at Work Study*, your generation has a sky-high preference for learning by using tools and applying knowledge in real time. You don't just download new apps, you master them faster than most people can find the user manual. You prefer practical, action-based learning, and you're energized by environments where you can test, tweak, and iterate.

What makes this such a powerful edge? You thrive in fast-evolving industries, especially AI, SaaS, digital design, and marketing tech, where staying ahead depends on your ability to learn, adapt, and teach others.

> "Your generation isn't just talking about a better future: you're actively building it, leveraging technology to create solutions that matter."
> **—Dan Negroni**

Whether it's onboarding your team onto a new AI tool, streamlining workflows through automation, or setting up a low- or no-code product prototype, you bring practical innovation to life. You're not waiting for a permission slip to experiment.

Purpose-driven and inclusive

Your generation has a 48% higher preference for creating inclusive, human-centered workplaces compared to earlier generations. You show a strong preference for belonging and openness, which translates into two distinct advantages:

- You build connection through contribution. You don't just want to feel good at work, you want to do good.

- You thrive in diverse environments where different perspectives lead to better outcomes.

"For there is always light, if only we're brave enough to see it.
If only we're brave enough to be it."
—**Amanda Gorman, poet and activist**

Even as political climates shift, the Workverse is still being shaped by a growing global focus on sustainability, inclusivity, and social accountability, and your generation's strengths put you right at the center of it. You're not just motivated by purpose: you act on it, using your values to guide what projects you say yes to and who you want to work with.

"I used to think passion projects had to be separate from work. But the more I leaned into roles where I could lead change, the more energized I felt, even on Mondays."
—**Laila, 22, public policy associate**

Connection via a digital world

Unlike earlier generations, who lean heavily on meetings or calls to collaborate, Gen Z has a 47% higher preference for reading and writing as the most effective way to connect, collaborate, and make decisions.

That means you're at your best in async-first environments, where tools such as Slack, Notion, and Microsoft Teams allow you to contribute on your own terms. You prefer clarity over chatter and reflection over reaction.

This also makes you a natural fit for hybrid or distributed teams. You bring process, clarity, and thoughtful communication that cuts through noise. Your ability to explain things clearly, without having to be the loudest voice in the room, is a powerful strength. You engage deeply, reflect independently, and contribute meaningfully.

Your problem-solving superpower

The Gen Z at Work Study found that your generation has a 23% higher motivation to solve problems compared to earlier generations, who prefer to chase long-term aspirational goals. You're less about big visionary slogans and more about *fixing real problems right now.*

While some generations light up over the idea of "being the next Airbnb of X," you're the one asking *What's broken? How do we build a better fix and make sure it lasts?* You find your drive solving urgent challenges like "Cutting global carbon emissions by 50% before 2030." Both paths create impact; they just get there differently.

It's a grounded, prevention-focused mindset, one that channels energy into predicting issues, spotting risks early, and addressing challenges before they spiral. In the Workverse, this way of thinking is prized: workplaces need people who can anticipate problems and keep systems strong. And the data backs it up: across every region, human skills like problem-solving are in significantly higher demand than digital skills.[32]

> "I used to feel guilty about not getting excited by our CEO's grand vision talks. Then I realized my focus on fixing security vulnerabilities was protecting that vision. Different people contribute different pieces to the puzzle."
> —Jordan, 23, software developer

But not every problem needs to be solved at speed; one of your generation's most overlooked strengths is knowing when to pause, wait, and reflect.

Reflection and patience: Slowing down to see clearly

Not every solution is about moving fast. Sometimes the real power lies in slowing down. *The Gen Z at Work Study* found that your generation has a very high bias and motivation for reflection and patience. That means you're comfortable pausing, observing, and letting ideas settle before leaping into action.

In many contexts, this rhythm is a strength, not a weakness. It gives you space to understand the real problem—not just the symptom—before you start solving. It also helps you notice voices and perspectives that others might overlook in the rush to "move fast and break things."

For many of you, this way of working feels more organic and connected to the world around you. It mirrors ecological cycles and Indigenous knowledge systems that value seasons, land, and slowness as forms of intelligence. It's a counterbalance to hustle culture: change that is thoughtful, systemic, and deeply inclusive. From work seasons to climate seasons, you already know life doesn't move in straight lines; it moves in cycles.

Reflection and patience let you ask *When is the right time to act? Are we considering everyone impacted?* This approach not only leads to better solutions but also to workplaces that feel more sustainable and human.

> "When I stopped trying to chase every opportunity and gave myself time to reflect, I realized I wanted work that heals, not just work that hustles."
> **—Amira, 24, sustainability graduate**

Your generation's ability to hold space, sit with complexity, and wait for the right moment to act is a superpower in its own right. Combined with your problem-solving drive, it means you're wired to create change that lasts, not just change that's fast. This isn't just stepping back, it's stepping differently. And it's how your generation is wired to create systemic change. It's about setting a rhythm that makes your energy and your impact last.

Detail-oriented thinking: Your precision is a power-up

While earlier generations excel at painting with broad strokes, you have an unprecedented ability to spot nuances others overlook. It's like having a built-in microscope: you can catch what others miss, raising the standard for everyone around you. Gen Z raises the bar when it comes to clarity and detail, and you thrive when the brief is clear, the expectations are defined, and there's a way to measure success.

Your generation's motivation for clarity and specifics is 120% higher than earlier generations. You're not nitpicking, you're quality-controlling. You catch the bug in the code, the loophole in the policy, the typo in the pitch deck before anyone else sees it.

Analytical thinking and precision are among the most in-demand skills for the future of work. So while someone might tease you about triple-checking that spreadsheet, you're cultivating one of the most in-demand capabilities in today's workplace. In industries such as finance, healthcare, cybersecurity, and consulting, this trait is gold. But it also shines in creative fields, where precise execution makes a bold idea real.

You've just explored seven of the most powerful motivational strengths Gen Z brings to the Workverse. In Chapter 7, we'll go even deeper, so you can explore your own unique mix and learn how to use it to your advantage.

Where your superpowers shine brightest

Back in Chapter 4, we explored the most in-demand roles of the future. Here's the good news: the very environments where Gen Z thrives—collaborative, purpose-driven—are the same ones powering those roles forward.

Whether it's sustainability, AI, digital design, or inclusive leadership, your motivational edge gives you a head start. Your Workverse sweet spot isn't just where you can work; it's where your natural preferences, strengths, and ways of thinking make you stand out.

Here's how:

- Your attention to detail gives you an edge in compliance-heavy roles such as finance, insurance, and cybersecurity.

- Your collaboration and problem-solving mindset make you invaluable in cross-functional product, design, and ops teams.

- Your digital fluency helps you lead in SaaS, AI, and martech, where tools evolve weekly and onboarding needs to happen fast.

- Your purpose-driven values position you to thrive in sustainability, impact investing, or regenerative industries.

- Your patience and reflection give you an edge in solving the toughest challenges that need long-term, systemic thinking.

> "Real impact comes from actions measured by lasting change, not temporary applause."
> **—Dean Foley, Australian Kamilaroi man and entrepreneur**

Your motivational strengths don't just *align* with the Workverse—they help shape it, with a pace that's sustainable as well as innovative.

Explore your Gen Z edge

You've just explored Gen Z's collective strengths. Now it's time to bring the focus back to *you*. Your mix of traits will be different from even your closest friends: no two motivational fingerprints are alike. This is where self-awareness becomes a real game-changer.

See how your strengths line up with your generation's superpowers

Marlee helps you compare your unique motivations with the broader Gen Z picture. It's like holding up a lens: you'll see where you align with your generation's edge, and where you bring something entirely your own. Head to Marlee.com, log in, go to *Boards*, and create your *Gen Z and Me* Board: your personal visual snapshot that shows how your motivations stack up against your generation.

How to use it

Step 1: Check your motivational matchups

Explore your highest and lowest motivators. Which Gen Z strengths do you share? Where do you stand out? Click *Generate Insight* to see your personal comparison come to life.

_____

_____

_____

Step 2: Dive into your patterns

Click into each motivation group and explore what it reveals.

- Do you get more energy from initiating things or taking time to reflect first?
- Do you thrive most when you're collaborating with people, or when you're hands-on with tools?
- Do you feel grounded by shared goals, or more alive when working independently?

Use *Generate Insight* for a tailored debrief that helps connect the dots.

_____

_____

_____

Step 3: Reflect on what this means for work

Ask yourself:

- Where do my strengths give me a natural edge?
- What kind of team, role, or environment brings out my best?
- What drains me, and what refuels me?

_____

_____

_____

_____

> "When you understand your natural strengths,
> you can design a work life that energizes you."
> **—Coach Marlee**

It doesn't matter whether your results match every Gen Z finding or differ entirely. Self-awareness is your superpower. The clearer you are on what drives you, the easier it becomes to choose roles, projects, and teammates that actually fit *you*.

Up next: Play to your strengths

You've just uncovered the motivational superpowers your generation brings to the Workverse, and maybe even started noticing which ones feel like yours.

"Success comes not from forcing yourself into traditional molds, but from finding environments where your authentic motivations become valuable assets."
—Michelle Duval

✳ ✳ ✳

Up next: We'll help you go deeper—mapping your unique combination of work preferences, energy drivers, and traits—so you can lead with confidence, communicate your value, and build a work life that energizes you on your terms.

CHAPTER 7

Play to Your Personal Strengths

TL;DR

Why discovering how *you* work best is your ultimate edge.

When you know what energizes you, you stop contorting to *fit in* and start shaping a Workverse where your strengths feel at home.

- **Your work environment matters:** do you thrive in a solo space, or feel energized by working around others?
- **What holds your attention:** tools, people, or systems reveal what motivates you.
- **How you make decisions:** knowing your decision-making style helps you design better ways of working and share them with your team.
- **Change vs. routine:** do you thrive on stability, or feel energized by variety?
- **Your *Individual Results Board*:** maps the patterns that reveal your strengths.

See the talent only you bring to the Workverse

You've probably been told to "know your strengths" a hundred times by now: on LinkedIn posts, in school workshops, maybe even by your manager. But what does that actually look like in your day-to-day work life? And how do you even begin to name what you're great at when most job descriptions are built for someone else's path?

Your personal strengths are more than just a bullet point on your CV. They're how you make decisions. How you get things done. How you bring energy to your team. And when you understand what truly drives you, that's when you gain the confidence to go after high-impact roles, write compelling cover letters, speak up in interviews, negotiate for what you're worth, or even build something entirely your own.

> "Exploring and naming your strengths invites you into an incredible journey of unique expression, evolution, and personal impact."
> —Michelle Duval

In the last chapter, we explored Gen Z's collective edge: the traits that stand out across your generation. But now it's time to focus on you. Because even if the data shows Gen Z tends to prefer structure or shared responsibility, that doesn't mean you do. Your personal work style—what we call your *motivational fingerprint*—might look very different. And that's not just okay. It's your superpower.

> "Different is good. When someone tells you that you are different, smile and hold your head up and be proud."
> —Angelina Jolie, global humanitarian, actor, and director

Now let's get practical: your motivations

See what drives how you think, work, and thrive, and how to use it

As we introduced in Chapter 1, motivations are your unique preferences that shape how you focus, make decisions, and tap into energy. When you can name them, you gain a decoder key for self-awareness. Instead of squeezing into someone else's definition of success, you can design a Workverse where your strengths naturally fit.

In this chapter, we'll walk you through the key motivational groups. Once you've taken the Marlee *Motivational Analysis*, these groups help you make sense of your results, connect the dots, and design a work life that fuels you instead of draining you.

> "Don't try so hard to fit in, and certainly don't try so hard to be different . . . just try hard to be you."
> —Zendaya, actor and producer

Do you thrive solo or as a team player?

This isn't about introvert vs. extrovert. It's about how you make decisions, take ownership, and feel energized in your day-to-day workflow.

Some people thrive when they're trusted to steer the ship solo, even when the water's rough. Others feel strongest when they're working in sync with teammates, co-creating solutions, building alignment, and making sure no one's left behind.

These styles show up in your *Responsibility* preference: either a strong drive to own a body of work yourself (*Sole Responsibility*) or a preference to share ownership and co-lead (*Shared Responsibility*).

Where this becomes your edge:

- **Sole Responsibility:** You may thrive in sole founder roles, strategy, consulting, or freelancing, anywhere your ability to run with ideas is seen as leadership.

- **Shared Responsibility:** You shine in product teams, people and culture, agile sprints, or collective organizations where mutual accountability is key.

"When I'm the only one accountable, I feel more focused. But in team sprints, I get more creative. Knowing the difference helped me shape my hybrid role to match both sides."
—Daria, 24, project analyst

Are you a vision-setter or a problem-solver?

Some people get energy from big goals: tracking progress, imagining future outcomes, and planning their moves months in advance. Others light up when there's a real-world issue to fix *right now*. You might be more energized by resolving a customer issue today than by mapping your five-year plan.

This shows up in the *Action Direction* motivational group:

- **Achieving Goals**: is about future vision and milestone progress.
- **Problem-Solving**: is about assessing risk now and in the future and fixing what's broken.

Where this becomes your edge:

- **Achieving Goals**: Project management, coaching, scaling operations, or sales roles that rely on targets and metrics.
- **Problem-Solving**: Engineering, policy reform, climate tech, or service delivery—spaces where you jump in and make things better, fast.

> "I used to think not being excited about OKRs meant I wasn't ambitious. But I realized I'm just more driven when there's a real issue to fix in front of me."
> —**Avi, 22, product support lead**

Let's talk about what sparks your attention at work

What truly captures your curiosity?

When you get stuck in a long task list, it's easy to forget what first drew you into a project in the first place. But deep down, we all have specific things we're drawn to, topics or themes that naturally hold our attention, no matter what's going on around us.

This is where your *Interest Filters* come in. These reveal what you're most curious about at work. And once you know it, you can start aligning your roles, projects, and learning paths to match.

> "When you figure out how you work best, no one can take that power away from you. That's what changes everything."
> —Dan Negroni

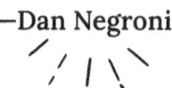

Here are the eight key interest areas. Which ones feel most like you? That's your edge.

- **People:** You're energized by human stories, relationships, and conversations. You likely thrive in coaching, people management, sales, customer experience, or community-building roles.

- **Tools:** You're drawn to using, improving, or mastering physical or digital tools. Think engineering, UX, product testing, or even artisan trades.

- **Systems:** You likely appreciate how things work together. Great for operations, logistics, product architecture, or anything involving complex coordination.

- **Information:** You're lit up by researching, organizing, and making sense of knowledge. Perfect for roles in data analysis, journalism, documentation, or research.

- **Money:** You're motivated by revenue, pricing, value creation, and financial levers. You'd likely enjoy roles in finance, startups, or any business-focused environment.

- **Place:** You care deeply about where things happen: cities, regions, cultures, and physical or conceptual environments. Urban planning, location strategy, tourism, or sustainability might resonate.

- **Time:** You're interested in cycles, timing, scheduling, and working with time. Ideal for project management, time management, scheduling, and planning.

- **Activity:** You love work that keeps you busy and active, where you're never idle.

"I've always been the one who experiments with new tools on my team. Last quarter, I introduced an automation that cut our reporting time in half. Now, people come to me when they need workflow improvements: it's become my unofficial role, and I love it."
—Felix, 24, data analyst

How do you best learn and communicate?

Everyone processes information differently. Some of us need to see a visual. Others need to hear it out loud, read it silently, or try it for ourselves. Recognizing how you learn best directly impacts your success at work.

These preferences are called *Convincer Input*, and they influence how you learn, collaborate, and are convinced.

- **Seeing**: Visuals, diagrams, dashboards.
- **Hearing**: Verbal walkthroughs, podcasts, conversations.
- **Reading**: Written docs, Slack threads, Notion pages.
- **Doing**: Hands-on learning, prototyping, trial and error.

Where this becomes your edge:

- **Seeing**: Great for UX/UI, marketing design, or data visualization.
- **Hearing**: Ideal for coaching, leadership, facilitation, or client engagement.
- **Reading**: Perfect for content strategy, legal, research, or documentation roles.
- **Doing**: Thrive in tech, fieldwork, service delivery, or engineering.

"I used to think my preference for Slack over impromptu desk visits was a weakness. Then my manager pointed out how my detailed written updates helped our global team stay aligned better than any video call could."
—Jamie, 29, software developer

How do you navigate change?

Your comfort with change can shape how you respond to innovation, growth, or even feedback. This shows up in the *Change* motivational group:

- **Sameness:** You like stability. You find your groove and stick to what works.

- **Evolution:** You enjoy small, steady upgrades. Familiarity with improvement.

- **Difference:** You crave variety and reinvention. New industries, new challenges.

Where this becomes your edge:

- **Sameness:** Systems roles, compliance, risk, or long-term client work.

- **Evolution:** Innovation, brand strategy, or continuous improvement.

- **Difference:** Startups, creative fields, R&D, or fast-growth environments.

> "I used to bounce jobs a lot and felt flaky. But when I reframed it as thriving in high-change roles, I finally found my place in a startup studio."
> —Santi, 23, venture builder

What's your style for making things happen?

Some people feel most confident following step-by-step procedures. Others prefer flexibility to explore multiple options. This is your *Task Direction* at play:

- **Procedures**: You prefer clear, linear steps.
- **Alternatives**: You like having options and figuring out your own path.

Where this becomes your edge:

- **Procedures**: Healthcare, finance, manufacturing, operations.
- **Alternatives**: Branding, content, entrepreneurship, or innovation labs.

How do you respond to rules and expectations?

This group helps you understand your relationship with the organizational structure, or *Rules*:

- **Assertiveness**: You believe your rules are good rules for everyone.
- **Indifference**: You do not see the world through the lens of rules.
- **Compliance**: You like to know and follow the rules closely.
- **Tolerance**: You're comfortable with diverse opinions and working styles.

Where this becomes your edge:

- **Assertiveness**: Activism, policy reform, campaigner.
- **Indifference**: Startups, creative industries, or async/remote-first cultures.
- **Compliance**: Legal, audit, risk, safety, or finance.
- **Tolerance**: Coaching, inclusion programs, diplomacy, multicultural teams.

Use your results to play to your strengths

Sometimes your strengths are easy to spot. Other times, they show up in ways you haven't fully recognized yet, like the quiet clarity you bring to team chaos, or your ability to spot patterns no one else notices. Your Marlee *Individual Results* Board helps shine a light on these motivators, so you can work in ways that feel more like you.

Whether you're just getting started or shifting directions, this is your personal roadmap. You can bring your strengths into sharper focus and start putting them to work.

Step 1: Visualize your personal strengths

Head into Marlee and open your *Individual Results* Board. You'll see your top motivations visualized, like a snapshot of what makes you tick. Hit *Generate Insight* for a deeper breakdown.

These insights are your fast-track to knowing where you shine and how to play to it. The Board is like a cheat sheet for your next role, project, or team.

_____

_____

_____

Step 2: Ask me about your strengths

Click *Ask Marlee* and type: "What are my strengths?" I'll walk you through how you make decisions, communicate best, and what work environments help you shine.

_____

_____

_____

Step 3: Put your strengths to work

- If you're motivated by solving problems, ask to shadow someone fixing a real challenge in your organization.
- If you love shared responsibility, co-create a task list with a teammate instead of working solo.
- If you prefer written input, take the lead on drafting a proposal, summary, or asynchronous update.

_____

_____

_____

_____

> "Small shifts lead to big momentum.
> Your strengths are here. Let's use them."
> —**Coach Marlee**

Now choose your path

By now, you've explored both the collective strengths of your generation and the deeply personal motivators that shape how you work best.

Up next: We'll take that insight and put it to work, helping you find environments, team structures, and new models of work where you'll thrive. Because when you know how you're wired, you stop guessing and start designing.

CHAPTER 8
Create and Build Your Path

TL;DR

Knowing your ideal work environment is just as important as knowing your strengths.

In a Workverse full of choices, the best-fit role won't come from scrolling; it'll come from understanding what environment brings out the best in you and designing around it.

- **There's no one-size-fits-all anymore:** you'll thrive when you align with the right work environment for you.
- **Supertemp and solopreneur paths offer freedom:** they also require clarity, accountability, and self-direction for you.
- **Hybrid models feel most natural to Gen Z:** when there's clear structure and async respect.
- **Networked collectives run on shared purpose:** just make sure you're aligned on values and norms.
- **The key is designing around your motivators:** your *Work Environment Board* can guide you.

Navigate the new world of work

You close your laptop after yet another LinkedIn scroll session, eyes glazing over job ads that blur together. Your group chat is buzzing: one friend just landed a hybrid role at a clean energy startup, another is juggling freelance design gigs and part-time bar shifts, while a third is moving to Bali to launch a wellness collective. Meanwhile, your family keeps asking, "So, have you figured out what you're doing with your life yet?"

No wonder your brain short-circuits. It's not that you lack ambition; it's that nobody explained how to navigate the wild variety of work environments emerging in the Workverse. And when you don't know where you thrive best, even the most exciting role can leave you drained.

This chapter is here to change that.

We've already unpacked the end of the traditional career ladder in Chapter 3 and mapped the industries where Gen Z is poised to thrive in Chapter 4. Now, we're exploring the environments where you'll do your best work: the systems, structures, and rhythms that fuel (or frustrate) you. Success in the Workverse isn't just about what you do—it's about where and how you do it.

> "If you're happy doing what you're doing, then nobody can tell you you're not successful."
> —**Harry Styles, singer and actor** 🎵

Let's explore four work models rapidly gaining traction and help you figure out how much of each one feels most aligned for you.

"The Workverse isn't a place you fit into; it's something you design. The real power move? Owning your choices and building a work life that reflects what energizes you."
—Dan Negroni

The supertemp ecosystem: Freedom and flexibility with AI-powered gig work

If you've ever thought, *Why am I expected to sit at a desk from nine to five when I could earn more doing outcome-based projects on my time?* You're not alone. As outlined in Chapter 5, many people are stepping away from traditional roles and embracing agile, high-impact project work. It's fast-paced, flexible, and designed for results, not hours.

"I started freelancing in college, just picking up small UX gigs to earn extra cash, but pretty quickly, I realized I didn't want to wait five years to work on meaningful projects.
I wanted freedom now. Within two years, I was earning more than my full-time friends, and choosing who I worked with, not just who hired me."
—Suzy, 24, UX designer

Supertemps are highly skilled individuals brought in on short-term contracts to deliver specific outcomes. Think fractional CMOs, AI ethicists, sustainability strategists, or product design leads. These aren't gig workers clocking in for task-based labor. They're respected collaborators who bring niche expertise and a track record of results.

What motivates Gen Z to explore (or avoid) this model?

Based on *The Gen Z at Work Study*, your generation tends to prefer stability and routine. So the fluid, rotating nature of project work might feel disorienting—especially at first—unless you develop rituals and practices that help you feel grounded, no matter where or who you're working with.

> "If your motivation dips when you're not anchored, build routines that travel with you."
> —Michelle Duval

That said, you're also big fans of tech-enabled tools and clear written communication: two superpowers that make async, independent work easier to manage once you've found your rhythm.

The real challenge? Many Gen Zers hesitate when they don't have a clear starting point. Without a boss checking in or teammates nudging you along, it's easy to stall. If you're drawn to this model, think about how you'll stay accountable without relying on external direction.

Feeling scattered or free? That depends on your systems

Do you light up at the thought of variety, or does it leave you scrambling? If outcome-based work excites you, you'll want to experiment with rhythms that ground you, like themed workdays, shared client templates, or mini-sabbaticals between contracts.

How can you experiment now

- Contract with one startup per quarter on fixed-term projects, then take two weeks off to reset your energy.

- Build a roster of two to three recurring clients who align with your values and offer repeat work: consistency fuels confidence.

- Use platforms such as Contra or Braintrust to test out project-based gigs without fully leaving your current setup.

Hybrid harmony: When structure and flexibility co-exist

If you've ever said, "I just want to work from home *some* days, but still feel like I belong to a team," then you're already thinking in hybrid terms. Hybrid models are no longer the fallback; they're the foundation for a huge portion of workplaces.

This structure blends remote independence with in-person connection. You might start your week checking in via Zoom, dive into focused async work mid-week, and gather at a co-working hub every Thursday for real-time strategy and collaboration. Done well, a hybrid work model isn't a compromise.

> "Hybrid works because it gives me just enough face time to feel like I'm part of something, but I still get space to focus. I've got a rhythm now. Mondays and Fridays at home, Wednesdays in the office, and the rest? I make it work around my energy."
> —Zion, 26, climate tech company

Why hybrid often feels like home to Gen Z

According to *The Gen Z at Work Study*, you tend to crave clear expectations, familiar routines, and a sense of shared connection. That's why structured hybrid setups work especially well when there's clarity around when to meet, how to communicate, and how progress is measured.

On the flip side, Gen Z is more likely to struggle when the hybrid model is vague, unstructured, or leaves you guessing. Environments where leaders say, "we're flexible," but never define what that means? This can cause ambiguity and even anxiety for your generation, and is where burnout and disconnection can sneak in.

Is your hybrid working *for* you, or just happening to you?

Before jumping into a hybrid role, dig into how the structure plays out. Are collaboration hours defined? Are communication norms clear? Do your teammates respect async boundaries, or are you expected to be online all day, every day?

> "Don't settle for vague. Find out how hybrid really works, then see if it works for you."
> —Dan Negroni

Want to try it out first? Here's how.

- Look for internships or project roles that offer hybrid flexibility with clear expectations.

- During interviews, ask specific questions such as "How does your team handle remote collaboration and feedback loops?"

- Test your own rhythm—try three days of remote work followed by one to two days of co-working or in-person meetups to see what energizes you.

Networked collectives run on shared purpose and decentralized power

Imagine collaborating on something meaningful with a group of independent creators: no titles, no hierarchies, no rigid organization charts. That's the essence of networked collectives: communities of people who team up around shared values, aligned missions, and mutual trust.

These collectives often leverage digital platforms to coordinate efforts across geographies. For instance, open-source software communities bring together developers worldwide to contribute to projects like LangChain, which enables modular AI application development, or Astro v3, revolutionizing frontend development with its "islands architecture." Decentralized Autonomous Organizations (DAOs) operate on blockchain technology, enabling members to make collective decisions without centralized leadership. Creative cooperatives, such as artist-run platforms, allow contributors to share ownership and decision-making responsibilities, fostering a sense of shared purpose and equity.

You might contribute to an open-source climate tech project. Or join a design collective where revenue is split among contributors. Or show up weekly in a Web3 community, solving real-world problems with decentralized tools. In these spaces, there's no single "boss"; everyone is there to build together.

> "When I joined my first collective, I finally felt like I wasn't working for someone; I was building with people.
> We choose our roles, and we decide how to contribute.
> It's all opt-in. It feels way more human."
> —Mateo, 25

Why this model resonates with Gen Z's values

According to *The Gen Z at Work Study*, you're deeply motivated by connection, belonging, and purpose. Traditional hierarchies often feel too rigid or impersonal, whereas collectives are about collaboration over control.

That said, the lack of a clear structure can sometimes create friction for Gen Z. If you rely on routines or clear role definitions, collectives may feel chaotic unless strong community norms are in place. The upside? When the mission is clear and the vibe is right, you'll likely feel more energized than in top-down teams.

It's all about culture alignment and energy alignment

Before diving into a collective, ask yourself, *Is the mission meaningful to me? Do I understand how decisions are made? Are roles flexible but still clear*? The answers to these questions matter way more than whether it "sounds cool" on paper.

> "Shared purpose is powerful, but don't mistake chaos for freedom."
> —Michelle Duval

Want to dip your toe in? Start small

- Join a community call for a DAO or creative collective and listen before jumping in.

- Offer to contribute to a single project or sprint before committing long-term.

- Pay attention to how the group handles communication, feedback, and follow-through. It'll reveal whether it's sustainable or draining.

> "I contribute to multiple DAOs, choosing projects I'm passionate about while earning across different industries. It's the ultimate work-life freedom."
> —Aiden, 26, UX designer

AI solopreneurs: Building it your way (but not going it alone)

Maybe you've had this moment: you're staring at your favorite creator's "I just made $10K this month" post while sitting in your third team call of the day, wondering, *Could I just go out on my own?* From AI-powered content creation to automated e-commerce, new tools allow AI solopreneurs to scale businesses with minimal overhead, handling everything from customer service to marketing without hiring employees. Solopreneurship is becoming a serious option for Gen Zers who crave freedom, autonomy, and creative control.

From YouTube editors to AI course builders to niche e-commerce brands built on TikTok, Gen Z solopreneurs are designing businesses that reflect their personal values and lifestyles. You don't need a co-founder or a funding round to start. Just an idea, a skill, and a space online to test it.

> "I launched my own studio because I needed control over my time and creativity. But I had to learn fast—things like pitching myself without cringing or saying no to clients who didn't respect my boundaries. You grow up quick when there's no safety net."
> —Zaria, 23, graphic designer

Why this model can be both empowering and draining

If you love independence and want to build something on your own terms, this model might sound like a dream. But here's what *The Gen Z at Work Study* reveals: while many of you value freedom, you also tend to avoid overly complex structures, and struggle when there's no one to check in with. You're more comfortable with practical tools and step-by-step clarity than chasing big abstract visions alone.

So while AI solopreneur life offers control, it also demands consistency, self-direction, and commercial confidence, traits that don't always come naturally to many Gen Zs. Many Gen Zers underestimate just how much marketing, planning, and decision-making are involved when you're the only one at the table.

Designing a solo setup that works for you

Ask yourself, *Do I thrive in solitude, or do I need feedback and social energy to stay focused? Am I building something because I love the work, or am I just trying to escape a bad job setup?* Your answers will shape how sustainable solopreneurship really feels for you.

> "Build in feedback loops. You don't have to do everything alone just because you're the boss."
> —Dan Negroni

Want to start without burning out? Here's how

- Launch a micro-offer—a simple one-page service or digital product—and test it with a small audience first.

- Block time weekly for admin, marketing, creative, and recovery. Don't treat rest as optional.

- Find or build a peer circle of other solopreneurs where you can trade wins, gut checks, and ideas without pressure.

"My store runs 80% autonomously, so I focus on growth and strategy. AI handles the operations."
—**Steven, 25, startup founder**

Match your motivations to work environments

You've now explored four environments shaping work. But reading about them isn't enough; you need to know which one actually fuels you. When you uncover how your motivations line up with your surroundings, you stop guessing and start building a work life that feels like it fits.

Step 1: Pinpoint what energizes you

Head to Marlee.com, log in, and create your *Work Environment* Board. As you explore your motivations, click *Generate Insight*: you'll start to see the conditions that bring out your best. Maybe it's the calm of structured systems, or the buzz of small collaborative teams. This is where clarity begins.

_____

_____

_____

_____

Step 2: Ask Marlee

Curious what this all adds up to? Click *Ask Marlee* and type: "What is the ideal work environment for me?" You'll get personalized guidance that cuts through the noise, whether you're built for fast-paced sprints, independent deep work, or something in between.

_____

_____

_____

_____

Step 3: Design your ideal work setup

Now take what you've discovered and turn it into a compass. Jot down two or three features you want in your work environment: like async communication, long project cycles, or a team that thrives on shared responsibility. These are your guardrails for evaluating roles, companies, and project offers.

_____

_____

_____

_____

_____

> "You don't need to have it all figured out. Just notice where your energy flows, and build from there."
> —Coach Marlee

Understanding your ideal work environment is important—it's the foundation of a work life that sustains your creativity, protects your energy, and amplifies your strengths. When your surroundings support your wiring, work stops feeling like a grind and starts feeling like a fit.

Bring it all together: Choose your environment, own your energy

You've now explored four models shaping the future of work and how to match them to your motivations. What you choose isn't a fixed identity. It's a sandbox. A playground. A system you can evolve and remix. Now go apply it to your Workverse.

What matters most is this: when your work environment aligns with your energy, everything gets easier. You feel more confident. More productive. More like yourself.

Up next: We'll help you take these insights and land dream opportunities that bring them to life. You'll learn how to spot roles that fit your unique work style and win them with confidence

CHAPTER 9
Land Your Dream Job Now

TL;DR

Why finding the right role starts with knowing your mission and treating the search like a full-time project.

Your dream job doesn't land by luck. It's found through self-awareness, strategic action, and aligned storytelling. This chapter gives you a full framework to find, tell, and land the role that energizes you.

- **Start with your mission and values:** they guide what energizes you and where you'll thrive.
- **Shortlist roles based on your motivators:** use tools such as Marlee and AI to spot patterns and fuel flow.
- **Search smarter, not wider:** focus on purpose-driven platforms, aligned environments, and strategic fit.
- **Tailor every application and story:** let your digital presence reflect your mission, not just your résumé.
- **Begin your role with purpose:** lead from day one with intention, reflection, and your unique strengths.

Make finding a job *your* job

Your dream job isn't found by chance. It's not a fluke, a lucky break, or a single magical opportunity that lands in your inbox.

People who land roles that they love treat job searching like a full-time, high-performance project. They don't leave it to luck; they create systems, test ideas, reflect often, and recalibrate. They make finding a job their job.

That might sound intense, but it works.

Research confirms that people who take a systematic approach, of setting clear goals, tracking progress, and tailoring their applications, are more likely to land interviews, receive offers, and improve their employment outcomes. Strategic planning and self-regulation are statistically correlated with higher success rates in the job market.[33]

But not all work environments work for Gen Z. According to *The Gen Z at Work Study*, this generation tends to prefer structure that's flexible, outcomes that align with their values, and tools that reflect how they learn and work best. Gen Z is generally less motivated by hierarchy or broad-stroke ambition, and more energized by meaningful alignment and adaptable systems.

That's why this chapter gives you a personalized, systematic, motivationally aligned process to help you:

- Stay clear on your mission

- Shortlist roles that match what drives you
- Use tech to work smarter (not just harder)
- Tell your story with purpose and precision

This is about creating a system to land the kind of role that fits now and evolves with you as you grow.

Let's start building that system now.

Ten steps to land your dream job

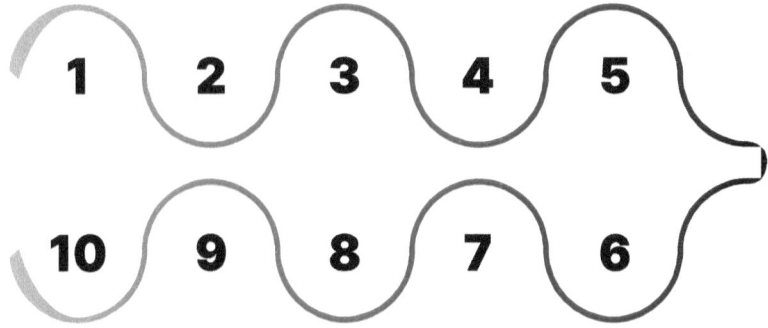

Why mission matters first

Before you hunt for job titles, start with something deeper— your mission.

Your mission isn't a grand vision or final destination. It's the direction that emerges when you follow what matters most to you: your values, your energy, and the impact you want to make.

For Gen Z, this is essential. You've grown up navigating climate shifts, digital transformation, evolving social norms, and a changing landscape of opportunity. You're not just asking, *What job should I take?* You're asking, *What kind of contribution do I want to make, and where do I start?*

That's what a mission is. It's not about having all the answers. It's about noticing the clues already showing up in your life.

Look at how others have found theirs:

- **MrBeast scaled generosity**, turning algorithm-driven content into a force for global giving.
- **Greta Thunberg acted out of grief**, not clarity, and sparked a climate movement.
- **Emma Chamberlain made realness aspirational**, proving that self-expression can become service.
- **Malala Yousafzai turned survival into advocacy**, showing that a mission sometimes chooses you.

Each of these missions started small. None was perfectly planned. They evolved through action.

When you can name your mission—even in draft form—your job search becomes less about ticking boxes and more about finding fit.

And when you can't? You risk drifting into roles that drain you or take you further from the person you're becoming.

So in the next step, we won't ask you to figure it all out. We'll help you notice the patterns that are already forming. Your mission isn't out there. It starts here.

Step 1: Anchor in mission, not job titles

You don't have to have a mission. You just have to notice one forming.

All those people you just read about? Their missions didn't show up as lightning bolts. They showed up in quiet patterns, difficult moments, or things they couldn't stop caring about.

So if you're wondering *Where do I start?* Start where your energy goes when no one's watching.

Ask:

- *What breaks my heart and makes me want to help?*
- *What do I keep returning to, even when it's hard?*
- *What kind of world would I secretly love to help build?*

Your mission is a direction. You're not *choosing* it—you're tuning in to what's been choosing you all along.

"You don't have to figure it all out right now. Let's start by listening—really listening—to the moments that move you. Your mission isn't something to chase. It's something you uncover by paying attention to what keeps calling you back."
—Michelle Duval

Mission is the shape your life takes when you're aligned.

Instead of scrolling job boards, hoping something will click, ask:

- *What lights me up so much that I lose track of time?*

- What's the pattern of contribution I keep returning to—teacher, protector, builder, advocate?

Remember, as we explored in Chapter 7, your Marlee *Individual Results Board* reveals these recurring clues. Instead of guessing, you can see them clearly in your motivations.

Curious where that might lead? Open the *Ask Marlee* feature and type:

- "What job would make me most happy?"

You'll get tailored insights that connect your energy to real roles, so you're not just daydreaming: you're starting from data.

. . . .

Bring it to life → Take action now:
See the patterns that point you toward your mission.

- Head to Marlee.com, log in, and click your avatar to open My Profile & Results → All Motivations → View Bubbles.

- Notice which motivations light up for you: their patterns are clues to the kind of work that will feel most energizing.

. . . .

Take notes on the motivational patterns that stand out.

_____

_____

_____

_____

_____

Step 2: Let values be your compass

If your mission is the direction, your values are the map.

Are you here to dismantle systems, heal communities, design new tools, or amplify unheard voices? When your mission and values align, work flows. When they don't, it drains.

Ask:

- *What do I stand for, and does my work reflect that?*

Again, you don't need to figure out your values in one sitting, but tuning in is one of the most powerful places to start.

Most people notice their values in real moments—when something feels deeply right or undeniably wrong. Your values live in your gut-level reactions: how you respond, what you choose, and what you resist.

Let's make it real by looking at the people we've just explored:

- **MrBeast's choices reflect a deep value for impact and abundance:** he didn't just want to succeed; he wanted others to succeed with him.

- **Greta Thunberg showed us that valuing truth and justice sometimes means standing alone.** Her courage was about conviction.

- **Emma Chamberlain built a platform on emotional honesty and freedom.** Her value of authenticity gave others permission to be fully themselves.

- **Malala Yousafzai's advocacy reveals values such as education and dignity.** Even when her path was shaped by crisis, she chose to respond with purpose.

So what about you?

"You don't need a list of perfect traits. Just ask: When was I proud of how I showed up? When did I feel out of alignment, and why? Your values are already there. Let's name them." —**Dan Negroni**

Try this reflection:

- *What actions or decisions have made me proud, quietly, even if no one saw them?*

- *When something felt unfair or off at work or school, what value was being crossed?*

- *What qualities do I most admire in others? What do they protect, fight for, or stand in?*
- *If someone watched my life for a week, what values would they see in action?*

Use these reflections to write down three to five core values you feel strongly connected to. They don't need to be permanent. But they can guide how you show up today.

_____

_____

_____

_____

_____

Bring it to life → Take action now:
Turn your values into clarity you can act on.

- Head to Marlee.com, and go to *Ask Marlee*. Type: "What do I uniquely contribute to my team?" You'll see your contribution framed through the lens of your strengths: often in ways you haven't put into words yet.

- If you would like to experience a personal coaching program to guide you through your values, personal mission, and vision, you can explore *Coaching → Start the Goal Catcher* program. It's designed to help you uncover the values behind your choices—whether that's freedom, justice, connection, or growth—so your decisions stop being random and start being values-led.

Step 3: Shortlist work that fuels your flow

With your mission and values as your compass, let's see what roles, industries, and environments energize you.

Think back over the last month: when did you feel switched on, at work, at uni, or in a side project? Time flew, energy was high, and distractions disappeared. Note down three of those moments. Maybe it was leading a group project, diving deep into research, or fixing a problem that no one else spotted.

Now, look for the pattern. What do these moments have in common? That's your clue to where you'll thrive, not just survive.

Bring it to life → Take action now:
Turn your motivations into work-life clues.

Try these two shortcuts:

Ask Marlee — prompts to use:

- "What motivates me?"
- "What work environments suit me?"
- "What roles suit me?"
- "What industries suit me?"

Ask ChatGPT — prompts to use:

- "What are five mission-driven roles that blend [insert your top motivations]?"
- "What industries are best suited to someone motivated by [insert your top motivations]?"

Here's an example of how motivations map to real-world roles: use it as inspo for your own list.

My top motivational traits	Aligned roles / industries / work styles
High Initiation	Startups, consulting, campaign work
Group Environment	Team-based roles, agile work models
Detail-Oriented (Procedures)	Ops, QA, project coordination
Present-Focused	Real-time problem-solving roles
People Interest	Community orgs, HR, coaching

_____

_____

_____

The goal is to notice patterns. When your work reflects your motivations, it becomes easier to stay energized, even when it's challenging.

Step 4: Build a system that adapts with you

The goal of this step is simple: create a repeatable way to test, track, and refine your job search so you're not guessing. A system is what turns your intentions into progress. It's the structure that keeps you consistent, shows you what's working, and helps you adjust when things change.

Without a system, it's easy to fall into panic mode: scrolling endlessly, sending the same résumé 50 times, and hoping something lands. That's noise. A system gives you focus: it helps you explore opportunities, notice patterns in your energy, and recalibrate as you grow.

Think of it like this:

- Your mission is your why.
- Your system is your how.

With a system, you're not just throwing résumés into the void; you're building a rhythm that keeps you energized and learning as your path unfolds.

Here's how to turn your search into a system you can trust:

- **Map it:** Use tools such as Notion AI, Trello, or a whiteboard to keep a running board of roles, orgs, and growth areas you're curious about.

- **Track patterns:** Each week, jot down what gave you energy and what drained you. Over time, you'll see what fuels your flow.

- **Test ideas:** Join a weekend hackathon. Volunteer. Build a portfolio piece in public. These small experiments give you fast feedback on what fits.

- **Recalibrate regularly:** Once a month, pause and ask, *What do I know now that I didn't last month?* Let those insights steer your next move.

> "Clarity isn't found all at once; it's built through action, reflection, and momentum."
> —**Michelle Duval**

Focus on building a system you can rely on: one that adapts with you and keeps you energized even when the path shifts.

....

Bring it to life → Take action now:
Turn scattered job ideas into a system you can trust.
- Head to Notion AI and open the *Job Application Tracking Template*. It'll help you organize roles, track progress, and keep your search feeling clear and manageable as you grow.

....

Jot down what you're learning

_____

_____

_____

_____

Step 5: Tell a digital story that matches your mission

This is where your strategy starts to show. Think of your digital presence as a living, breathing portfolio—not just a list of roles, but a reflection of your *why*. It's how the world glimpses what matters to you, what you're building, and where you're headed next.

> "I used to think LinkedIn was just for job titles and brag posts. But once I rewrote my profile to tell the story of why inclusive design matters to me, things changed. I started getting DMs from companies working on accessibility and purpose-driven tech."
> **—Zoe, 22, UX Designer**

That's the power of alignment. When your digital story reflects your mission, you start attracting opportunities that *fit*, not just roles that look good on paper.

Your key assets (and how to use them wisely)

Asset	Tool or platform	Pro tips to maximize it
CV/résumé	Kickresume, Rezi, ResumAI	Use ChatGPT to compare job descriptions to your résumé and adjust your tone to match mission-led language. Focus on *impact*, not just tasks.
LinkedIn	LinkedIn AI Writer, Marlee	This is a story, not a summary. Let your headline and *About* section reflect your mission and values, not just your current job title.
Portfolio/bio site	Typedream, Notion, Carrd	Go beyond aesthetics. Share real projects and explain *why* they matter. What problem did you solve? What did you learn?
Social media presence	Canva, Buffer, Threads	Show your voice and values consistently. Your posts don't have to be polished—just real. Share behind-the-scenes progress, not just polished wins.

Step-by-step social media refresh

Once your portfolio is in motion, make sure your social channels tell the same story so you're showing up with intention. Here's how to align your digital presence with your mission:

- **Choose your platforms:** Use each one for its strength. LinkedIn = professional story. TikTok = creativity or niche. Instagram = visual brand. Twitter/Threads = values and thoughts.

- **Update your bios:** Keep them simple, consistent, and mission-led. Try: "Designing inclusive systems that help teams thrive."

- **Post with purpose:** Share behind-the-scenes lessons, projects in progress, or reflections on what you're learning. These micro-stories say more than any job title.

- **Audit your past:** Take a scroll. Archive anything that no longer reflects your energy, values, or voice.

This is about letting your next opportunity *see you clearly*—mission, momentum, and all.

• •

Bring it to life → Take action now:
Show up on LinkedIn with a story that stands out

- Jump into your Marlee *Individual Results* Board, spot the traits that make you unique, and update your LinkedIn About section with one line that reflects them. It's a quick way to let future opportunities see your mission and momentum, not just your job titles.

• •

Note what needs a refresh

_____

_____

_____

Step 6: Search smart (and purposefully), not just widely

Scrolling endlessly through job boards can feel like looking for meaning in the comments section—noisy, chaotic, and mostly unhelpful. Instead of waiting for the perfect job post to appear, flip your strategy: search for aligned missions.

Start with platforms designed for purpose-driven work: Otta, Escape the City, TechLadies, Wellfound. These spaces make it easier to find teams building something that matters to the world and to you.

Search by cause, not just company. Look for roles connected to what energizes you—whether it's climate justice, equity in healthcare, mental well-being, or ethical tech. Filter by values, not just job functions.

Here's a shortcut: drop a job description into ChatGPT and ask:

- "What values and work style are embedded in this job description?"

You'll get insights into whether the team favors speed over process, autonomy over collaboration, or short-term impact over long-term vision. Pair those clues with your Marlee motivations to check whether the role really aligns with how you're wired.

Then ask yourself the bigger question:

- *Would this let me grow into the person I want to become?*

Because the best job isn't just a match for where you are—it's a launchpad for where you're headed.

Jot down roles that feel like a fit

_____

_____

_____

_____

Step 7: Customize your application for every role

Found an opportunity that aligns with your mission? Great. Now it's time to show up with intention, on paper and online.

Most employers today—especially in larger organizations—use Applicant Tracking Systems (ATS) to screen résumés before a human ever sees them. So, how do you stand out without selling out?

Use AI to tailor and optimize your application

Let smart tools do the heavy lifting while you stay focused on authenticity.

Start with a ChatGPT prompt: Paste your résumé and the job ad into ChatGPT and ask:

- "What keywords should I add to make my résumé more relevant to this role?"
- "Rewrite this bullet point to better reflect the qualifications in this job description."

This helps you speak the same language as the employer, without compromising who you are.

Try tools such as ResumAI or Jobscan: They'll score your résumé for ATS compatibility and show where to tighten alignment. Think of it like fine-tuning your signal so the right orgs hear it loud and clear.

Mirror their language, strategically: If the job ad says "cross-functional collaboration", don't write "worked well in teams." Small shifts in phrasing matter. Match the tone and keywords they use, while staying grounded in your voice and values.

Ask ChatGPT to review your résumé:

- "Act as a recruiter and review this résumé for a Gen Z applicant applying to [role]. What would you change to make it stand out?"

AI can help you beat the bots. But your mission—your why—is what resonates with people. So let the tools support your clarity, not replace it.

List the résumé versions you'll tailor for different roles

_____

_____

_____

_____

Step 8: Interview from the inside out

An interview isn't a test; it's a two-way conversation. You're not there to *prove* your worth. You're there to *share your energy* and explore whether this mission fits you too.

Start by getting comfortable in your own story. Tools such as Huru.ai or Google Interview Warmup can help you practice out loud without the pressure.

Focus on stories that show who you are, not just what you've done. Try stories such as:

- A moment where I led with my values
- A challenge I solved in my own way
- A time I realized: this work matters to me

Then, go deeper. Use Marlee to explore your motivational traits and how they show up in those moments. Maybe it's your drive to create change, your love of structure, or your ability to connect ideas others don't see. Whatever it is, name it, and own it.

When your answers come from the inside out, you're showing up—clear, confident, and grounded in your *why*.

Bring it to life → Take action now:
Turn your motivations into interview answers that stand out.

- Head to your Marlee *Individual Results* Board and pick two motivators that feel most "you." These will likely be in your top five motivations.

- Then, craft one short story for each, like how your love of structure helped a project succeed, or how your drive to solve problems made an impact.

- Practice sharing these out loud with a tool like Google Interview Warmup, so when the real moment comes, you're not scrambling, you're ready.

Jot down the stories you'll share

_____

_____

_____

_____

_____

Step 9: Know your worth and negotiate with confidence

You're not just looking for a "yes"—you're looking for a *whole-body yes*. One that feels right in your gut, not just your inbox.

Start by doing your homework. Use tools such as Levels.fyi, Blind, or Glassdoor to benchmark salary, benefits, and role expectations.

Then check in with yourself, because numbers are only part of the equation:

- *Will this support my energy and well-being?*
- *Will I still have time for rest, creativity, and real life?*
- *Is this a stepping stone toward my bigger mission, or a distraction from it?*

It's easy to slip into people-pleasing mode during negotiations. But don't trade alignment for approval. This is about *honoring the direction you're building toward.*

Your mission is worth protecting. And so are you.

Bring it to life → Take action now:
Check the facts, then check in with yourself

- Use Levels.fyi or Glassdoor to benchmark salary and benefits for your role.

- Then, open your Marlee *Individual Results* Board and reflect *Will this role fuel my motivations, or drain them?*

- Write down one non-negotiable (e.g., flexible hours, learning budget, supportive manager) to keep front of mind before you accept any offer.

Define what fair and energizing looks like

_____

_____

_____

_____

_____

Step 10: Start your role with purpose

Landing the role isn't the finish line; it's the next threshold. How you *begin* matters just as much as how you get there.

As you step into your new team, bring intention with you:

- **Refresh your LinkedIn or online profile** with a mission-aligned bio that reflects who you are, not just what you do.
- **Share reflections from your first month** through a post, a blog, or even a voice note on Threads. Let people in on what you're learning and why it matters.
- **Use your *Individual Results Board*** on Marlee to reset your energy plan and stay aligned with what fuels you.

And ask:

- *How can I embody my mission in this team from day one?*

When you lead with clarity, energy follows.

....

Bring it to life → Take action now:
Start your role with clarity, not guesswork.

- Log in to Marlee and revisit your *Individual Results* Board. Spot one motivation that fuels your best work, and set an intention to lean in and fully embrace any activities that support this motivation in your first 30 days.

- Pair it with a simple LinkedIn or Threads post about what excites you in this new chapter, so your team (and network) sees your mission, not just your title.

....

List the intentions you're setting
_____

_____

_____

Shape your work life with intention

Every step you take—from clarifying your mission to customizing your story—shows the world what energizes you, what matters to you, and how you'll make your mark. And even if you don't land the *perfect* role right away, you're building the skills, habits, and mindset to grow into it.

Next up: What happens when you don't feel fully ready? Chapter 10 is about closing the gaps that still feel tender. We'll explore how to turn your growth edges into fuel and grow into someone who's not just ready to land a dream role, but confident owning it and evolving with it.

CHAPTER 10

Go Grow Yourself

TL;DR

The fastest way to level up? Strengthen what doesn't come naturally, without changing who you are.

This chapter dives into the three most overlooked but work-life-shaping growth areas for Gen Z: big-picture thinking, initiative, and leadership influence.

- **Zoom out regularly:** big-picture thinking turns your daily tasks into long-term momentum.
- **Start before you're ready:** build initiative by acting fast and learning on the go.
- **Lead without a title:** own your influence by trusting your instincts and stepping up.
- **Focus your energy:** choose one growth area that would move the needle for you now.
- **Get support and track progress:** use tools such as Marlee's *Coaching* and the *Over Time Board* to stay in motion.

Unlock the skills that will set you apart

You know that feeling—you're putting in the effort, you're showing up, meeting deadlines, maybe even going above and beyond, but somehow, it's not translating into the progress you expected. You see others getting promotions, landing big projects, or becoming the go-to person in meetings, and you can't shake the feeling *What do they know that I don't?* Maybe you've heard feedback like, "You need to see the bigger picture" or "Take more initiative," but no one actually explains what that means. You're left wondering, *Okay . . . but how?*

From coaching so many of the world's most successful in their fields, here's a little secret: it's not just about working hard—it's about working in the right way. *The Gen Z at Work Study* found that there are three major areas where your generation can struggle—not because you're lacking talent (far from it), but because these skills require a different style of working than what generally comes naturally to your generation.

The three biggest growth opportunity areas? Big-picture thinking, taking initiative, and leadership influence. Embracing them is what helps you stand out and create a meaningful impact in your work life.

This isn't about identifying weaknesses. It's about understanding how you direct your energy. The way you approach different tasks at work isn't just about skill; it's about your attitude and motivation. Some things feel natural, like slipping into a comfortable pair of sneakers. Others feel like running in dress shoes—possible, but clunky and awkward. That's not because you're bad at them; it's because they can take a different kind of effort from you. And when something requires more energy, it's easy to assume, *maybe I'm just not good at this.* But that's not how growth works.

Growth isn't about forcing yourself to fit into someone else's definition of success. It's about developing skills in a way that works with your natural strengths, not against them.

And in a world where AI is automating routine tasks, skills such as big-picture thinking, initiative, and influence are what will add to your natural talent and set you apart. They're hidden keys that can unlock the next level of your work life.

And the best part: you don't have to change who you are to master them. You only need to refine how you approach them.

Let's break each one down

Why you need the bigger picture: Step back to see what matters

"Pioneers don't wait for permission. They don't follow maps; they draw them. Being first is scary because it's lonely and uncertain. But it's also exhilarating. If you want to leave a mark, you can't stick to well-worn paths. That's how you become a visionary."
—Kennedy Ekezie, entrepreneur, philosopher, and social advocate

The Gen Z at Work Study found that your generation is highly detail-focused but is not very motivated to see the bigger picture. In fact, compared to earlier generations, there has been a 53% decrease in big-picture, strategic thinking. That means you're driven to execute tasks with precision, but when it comes to stepping back and understanding the bigger *why* behind your work, it's not where your generation's energy naturally flows.

It's easy to get so caught up in your to-do list that you forget to ask, *Why does this task even matter?* When you're focused on execution, you can lose sight of how your work connects to a larger picture. And when that connection isn't clear, it can feel frustrating, like you're doing things just for the sake of doing them rather than contributing to something meaningful.

To thrive in your work life, it's important to bridge that strength into strategic awareness. Think of it like zooming in and out on Google Maps. If you stay zoomed in, you'll see streets and buildings, but you might miss the highway that connects everything. If you zoom out too far, you won't catch the details that make the difference.

Why does big-picture thinking matter in the Workverse?

Think of your work like a puzzle. If you focus only on one piece at a time, you'll place them correctly, but you won't see the full image forming, and importantly, you won't find the most efficient path to completing the puzzle. The bigger picture is how all the pieces connect, how your work influences company goals, and why certain strategies matter.

In the Workverse, those who can see beyond their immediate tasks are the ones who get promoted faster. They're the people who can anticipate problems before they happen, align their efforts with company priorities, and contribute to the larger conversation. They don't just *do* work; they shape it.

> "I see young employees working hard but not working smart. If you want to stand out, stop just completing tasks. Start understanding why they matter."
> —Jordan Lee, 35, senior recruiter, tech startup

The cost of big-picture blindness

If you're always head-down in the details, you miss opportunities—plain and simple. You might deliver solid work, execute projects with precision, and follow instructions perfectly. But if you never step back to understand the *why* behind your work, you'll struggle to see patterns, anticipate shifts, or recognize work-life-defining moments when they appear.

Think of it like grinding in a video game, completing quests, collecting rewards, and leveling up, but never checking the map to see where you're going. You might be progressing, but are you moving toward the right goal? If you don't pause to zoom out, you could spend months, or even years, doing great work that isn't leading you anywhere.

And here's another risk: you won't stand out to others who can help you succeed. When managers look for future leaders, they're not just looking for people who get things done—they want people who understand the bigger picture and contribute strategically. If you're just executing tasks without seeing how they fit into a broader vision, it becomes harder to make an impact beyond your current role.

Then there's burnout. When your work feels like an endless to-do list with no clear purpose, it starts to feel meaningless. You check things off, but it doesn't feel fulfilling because you don't see how your contributions matter. Over time, that's mentally exhausting. It's like running on a treadmill at full speed but never getting anywhere.

So, what happens if you don't fix this? You risk becoming invisible. You might be doing good work, but without big-picture awareness, you may be working on things that are just not the company's priority; you'll miss chances to shape strategy, get recognized, and advance faster in your work life.

So, how do you start to think bigger?

This can be a lot of fun. To build big-picture thinking, start playing "detective" at work. Ask more questions.

When you're assigned a project, don't just nod and get to work. Ask *How does this fit into the bigger goal? How does this connect to something bigger?*

If you're working on a report, don't just focus on formatting or data—ask how that information will shape a decision. If you're drafting an email, think about how it moves a project forward.

Observing strategic thinkers around you is another great way to develop this skill. Start observing the people who see the big picture effortlessly—usually managers and leaders.

How do they think? What kinds of questions do they ask? Who in your company always seems to anticipate what's coming next? Who isn't just reacting but shaping conversations?

Watch how they operate and start practicing that kind of thinking in your own work. Follow company-wide discussions, read about industry trends, and challenge yourself to think one level higher than what you're currently working on.

> "One of the most valuable things you can do is stop looking at tasks in isolation. Success comes from connecting ideas, not just completing checklists."
> —Dan Negroni

And here's a simple but game-changing habit: once a week, step back and ask yourself, *What's the larger priority or trend in my work?* It could be improving efficiency, supporting a bigger company shift, or contributing to a long-term goal. The more you practice zooming out, the clearer everything becomes.

Why overthinking holds you back: Taking initiative and moving fast

> "The key to success is to start before you're ready."
> —Marie Forleo, entrepreneur and author

The Gen Z at Work Study found that your generation has experienced a 44% decline in focus on initiation compared to earlier generations. While previous generations were more likely to jump into action quickly, Gen Z tends to pause, analyze, and seek certainty before making a move. This hesitation doesn't come from a lack of capability. It reflects the thoughtful, deliberate way your generation tends to approach action.

Initiation is the drive to start things independently and take quick action without waiting for permission or direction. People with high initiation are the ones who dive into new challenges, experiment before they have all the answers, and trust they'll figure things out as they go. Those with lower initiation, like many in Gen Z, prefer to gather information first, think things through, wait, and ensure they feel prepared before taking action.

This is a double-edged sword. Being deliberate can prevent mistakes, but waiting too long can mean missing out entirely. In today's Workverse, the biggest wins often go to those who move first and refine later.

Why does initiation matter in the Workverse?

Think about the difference between posting a TikTok and launching a YouTube channel. On TikTok, you record, hit post, and you're live—no overthinking, no endless editing. But launching a YouTube channel? That's a different beast. You might feel like you need the perfect camera, the right branding, and an ideal content strategy—so you spend months researching, tweaking, and second-guessing.

Meanwhile, someone else just started with an iPhone, bad lighting, and no clue what they were doing. Fast forward six months—their channel is taking off, and they're improving as they go while you're still waiting for the "right moment."

Your work is similar. You don't need to have all the answers before you start—you just need to get in the game.

Another way to think about it? AI is moving fast, and so should you. Companies aren't waiting for perfect AI policies before using ChatGPT, Midjourney, or Notion AI. They're experimenting, adapting, and figuring things out in real time. If you hesitate, the opportunity window shrinks while others jump ahead.

The cost of hesitating

Ever tried to grab concert tickets for your favorite artist, only to hesitate for just a moment too long? Maybe you wanted to check if the resale market would drop prices, compare different seats, or just think it over for a bit. And then suddenly . . . they're gone. Sold out. That hesitation didn't help—it cost you.

At work, waiting too long to act can have the same effect. While you're overthinking whether you should speak up in a meeting, someone else, maybe even someone less qualified than you, raises their hand and takes the opportunity instead. If you hesitate before volunteering for a project, a colleague steps in and gets the experience and recognition you could have had. If you don't raise your hand for an opportunity, someone with less experience but more initiative gets it instead.

Opportunities don't wait for you to feel ready. If you're always waiting for the perfect moment, you'll be waiting forever. The people who get ahead aren't necessarily the smartest or the most experienced—they're the ones who take action first and figure things out along the way.

And what about when you finally do feel ready? By that time, the moment may have passed. The project has been assigned, the promotion has been given, and the opportunity is gone. That's when you'll catch yourself thinking I *could have done that*, or *That should have been me*. In reality, it could have been, but you didn't step forward.

Hesitation keeps you stuck. It creates a pattern where you train yourself to wait instead of act, and the more you do it, the harder it becomes to break. The truth is, growth doesn't happen in a comfort zone. The only way to move forward is to push past the hesitation and take action before someone else does.

So, how do you start taking more initiative?

Shift your mindset from *Is this the perfect time?* to *What's the next small action I can take today?* Instead of waiting for every detail to be in place, challenge yourself to start messy and refine later.

Try the 24-hour rule: if you have an idea, take some kind of action within a day. Bring it up in a meeting, jot down an outline, or test a small version of it. Momentum beats perfection.

And the next time you feel that internal hesitation, remember this: speed wins. Whether it's social media, AI innovation, or work moves, the people who act first are the ones who get ahead.

> "You don't need permission to take action. The best way to prove your ideas work is to start and then refine as you go."
> 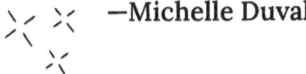 —Michelle Duval

That's exactly what Avi Schiffmann did when he was 17. When he saw that COVID-19 data wasn't being shared effectively, he didn't wait for someone else to fix it—he built one of the world's most visited tracking websites. Later, when the war in Ukraine broke out, he used the same approach to create a platform that helped more than 100,000 refugees find housing. He didn't wait for approval. He just started.

Why playing it safe holds you back: Building leadership and influence

The Gen Z at Work Study found that your generation has experienced a 40% decline in the motivation for power and influence compared to earlier generations. That means Gen Z is far less likely to seek leadership roles, step into authority, or position themselves as decision-makers.

At the same time, there has been a 60% decline in trusting your gut instinct for decision-making. Instead, Gen Z prefers to seek external validation, gather information, and wait for confirmation before making a move.

Leadership isn't just about titles or promotions—it's about influence. Influence means being the person who guides conversations, makes decisions, and drives action, regardless of job title. But if you always look outward for approval before making a move, you may struggle to step into leadership when it matters most.

One of the biggest misconceptions about leadership is that it's reserved for people with experience or authority. But leadership happens in everyday moments. It happens when you share an idea that sparks change. It happens when you help a teammate navigate a tough challenge. It happens when you step forward instead of waiting to be asked.

Paige Bueckers understood this when she used her platform as a basketball star to launch a foundation focused on youth sports and food security. She didn't wait for someone to tell her she was a leader. She created impact by taking action.

Why does influence matter in the Workverse?

If your GPS stopped working mid-route, what would you do? Some people would trust their sense of direction, remembering landmarks and navigating on instinct. Others would freeze, panicking without the reassurance of an external map. Leadership is a lot like that. If you always need a "map" (external input) before taking action, you'll hesitate when the moment requires decisive action.

One of the most underrated traits in leadership is the ability to trust your own judgment without constantly looking for outside input or permission. People with strong gut instincts listen to feedback but don't need constant reassurance before making decisions. They trust their gut, assess situations quickly, and move forward with confidence.

Right now, Gen Zers have a low preference for trusting themselves, meaning they might second-guess themselves, delay decisions, or look for someone else to take the lead. But leadership isn't given, it's taken.

> "Some younger employees wait for someone to tell them they're ready for more responsibility. The reality is, no one's going to hand it to you. You have to step up before you feel fully ready."
> —Jordan, 37, hiring manager

The cost of avoiding leadership

If you constantly wait for external feedback before making decisions, you might not even realize the hidden costs. Here's what happens when you don't step up:

You get overlooked, even when you're more capable than others

If you never actively put yourself forward for leadership opportunities, how will anyone know you're ready? Managers aren't mind readers. They assume that the people who step up want to lead, and they reward them accordingly. Meanwhile, you might be just as skilled (or even more capable) than the person getting the opportunity. But if you hesitate while they speak up, guess who gets noticed first?

You miss key moments to prove yourself

The best leadership opportunities don't always come with a formal invitation. They appear in small moments—a problem that needs solving, a project with no clear direction, a conversation where a strong opinion is needed. If you're always waiting for an official title before you take the lead, you'll miss the chance to prove your value before leadership roles are even on the table.

Your confidence never fully develops

The more you rely on outside validation, the harder it becomes to trust yourself. It creates a cycle: you hesitate, wait for reassurance, and then second-guess your instincts again. Over time, this trains your brain to believe that you always need someone else to confirm your decisions. But real confidence comes from experience, from making choices, taking action, and learning that you're more capable than you think.

Other people start shaping your work for you

When you don't actively shape your own path, someone else will. If you're not advocating for and trusting yourself, setting goals, and taking the lead in your own work life, your trajectory will be dictated by whatever projects get assigned to you, whoever decides to speak louder, or whatever is easiest for your boss to delegate. Leadership means owning your direction instead of passively following where others lead you.

You become dependent on external validation to move forward

If you always need feedback before making a decision, you'll struggle to trust your own instincts in high-pressure situations. The best leaders aren't reckless—they still listen to others—but they also know when to make a call, stand by it, and keep moving forward. If you're always checking for permission first, you risk becoming stuck in decision paralysis, especially when fast action is needed.

How do you start leading now?

The first step? Stop waiting for permission. If you want to build leadership skills, you have to start stepping up before you feel fully ready. The best leaders don't always have the perfect answer; they just make decisions with confidence and adjust as needed.

The next time you're in a meeting, make one decision without asking for reassurance. It could be proposing a direction for a project, giving your opinion without softening it with "I'm not sure, but...", or leading a discussion. The more you practice trusting yourself, the stronger your leadership instinct becomes.

And remember—leadership isn't about being the loudest in the room. It's about being the one who moves things forward. If you want to influence, you have to own your voice and use it.

 Your growth roadmap: Small shifts, big impact

You don't need to overhaul your entire work life to grow, just like you don't need a new engine to drive faster. Sometimes, it's a few strategic tweaks under the hood that unlock a whole new level of performance. Maybe it's shifting from idea mode to action mode faster. Maybe it's lifting your head to see the bigger picture. Or maybe it's learning to trust your own gut instead of crowdsourcing decisions.

Whatever it is for you, this next part is about taking the deep insights from this chapter and turning them into momentum. Because the goal isn't perfection—it's progress that sticks.

Step 1: Revisit your growth areas

Take a moment to reflect on which growth areas from this chapter feel like your biggest opportunity—big-picture thinking, taking initiative, or leadership. Think about recent situations at work where you felt challenged. Did you struggle to connect your work to a bigger goal? Did you hesitate to act on an idea? Did you avoid stepping up in a group discussion? Instead of seeing those moments as gaps, try looking at them as clear signs of where you can grow next.

Was it . . .

- Thinking more like a strategist? (*Big-picture thinking*)
- Starting before you're ready? (*Initiation*)
- Leading without needing all the answers first? (*Internal authority*)

Note the growth areas calling you

_____

_____

_____

_____

Step 2: Choose the one that moves the needle

Now, focus in. Which of those growth areas, if developed, would unlock the biggest wins in your current work life or future plans? Which one feels most urgent to unlock your next level?

_____

_____

_____

_____

"Even just naming what's holding you back can have a huge impact. That self-awareness becomes the lever that helps everything else shift."
—Coach Marlee

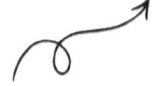

Once you've identified your focus, it's time to build momentum. Look back at the roles you were drawn to in Chapter 3. Are there patterns in what they require? If so, head back to Marlee.com, log in, and click *Ask Marlee* to type something like:

- "What are my blind spots for [strategy consulting]?"

You'll get a clear, personalized view of where you might stumble, and what to do about it. It's like having a mirror held up to the patterns you can't always see in yourself.

_____

_____

_____

_____

"Sometimes the fastest way forward is asking the right question. I'll help you unpack your answers—judgment-free."
—Coach Marlee

Step 3: Get the support you need to grow

You don't have to do this alone, and you're not expected to get it perfect the first time. Growth happens in layers. What matters is having the right support around you while you build confidence in the areas that feel harder right now.

That's why Marlee has created private and confidential AI coaching programs focused on the core areas Gen Z most often struggles with at work. Once you've logged in, head to the *Coaching* section of the Marlee.com app to explore programs and choose one that will have the biggest impact on your growth and momentum.

If strategic thinking felt like a gap for you, try the *Big Picture Thinker* coaching program. We'll walk you through practical ways to zoom out, spot patterns, and develop more strategic insight in your work life, without losing the detail you value.

If initiating faster is your growth edge, start with the *Start Fast* program. We'll help you flex your action muscle, move through hesitation, and build confidence in starting even before you feel ready.

And if growing into a more confident, influential leader is your next step, check out the *Personal Power* program. Together, we'll explore how to lead with more clarity, self-trust, and presence—on your terms.

List the programs that match your growth focus

_____

_____

_____

Each of these coaching programs is built around the real-world challenges Gen Z faces, not generic advice. We'll be with you every step of the way, helping you turn insight into action.

Step 4: Track your progress

To track your progress, think of it like leveling up in a game. You don't master every skill at once; you unlock them over time. Keep an eye on what's working, where you're stuck, and what adjustments you're making along the way. Growth isn't linear. But when you stay in motion, it compounds.

Want to visualize how far you've come? Create an *Over Time* Board in the Marlee.com app. It helps you see your growth mapped out across your motivational traits, so you can reflect on the shifts you're making and keep aiming forward with intention.

Jot down what's shifting over time

_____

_____

_____

_____

_____

Own your growth, then take it to the next level

You've probably noticed by now that growth isn't about forcing yourself into a mold. It's about understanding your strengths, knowing where to stretch yourself, and taking small, consistent steps forward. Start training yourself to think bigger, act faster, and lead with confidence, because the key is simply to begin. You don't need all the answers before you make a move. You don't need a perfect plan before you take the initiative. And you definitely don't need a title to start influencing the world around you.

If you're feeling stretched, good. That means you're expanding. And in today's Workverse, your ability to adapt, experiment, and grow on the fly is what will set you apart.

Growth isn't just about you. The next challenge? Learning how to navigate the people dynamics of work. Because no matter how sharp your skills are, your success will depend on how well you collaborate, communicate, and influence others.

Up next: We'll break down how to crack the collaboration code—so you can turn all of your personal growth into real momentum.

CHAPTER 11
Crack the Collaboration Code

TL;DR

Your technical skills get you in the door. But it's how you read the room that moves you forward.

This chapter is your guide to understanding the unspoken rules of teams—how communication, responsibility, and leadership really work across different generations and team setups.

- **Every team has two rulebooks:** learn both the formal structure and the unspoken norms.
- **Different generations = different playbooks:** match your communications to how others process, decide, and communicate.
- **Influence isn't about volume:** it's about knowing how to make your message land with different people.
- **Avoid friction with curiosity:** ask how others like to work, give feedback, and make decisions.
- **Ask Marlee and use Marlee Boards to decode team dynamics:** build trust faster, even in global teams.

The skill no one teaches (but everyone notices)

You've probably been told to "be a team player." But what does that actually mean?

In today's Workverse, working on a team doesn't always mean sitting in a meeting room, brainstorming ideas on a whiteboard. Your team might be spread across time zones, collaborating through shared docs, group chats, or AI teammates. You might never meet your manager in person, or find yourself trying to decode a coworker's emoji-only Slack message while wondering *Did I do something wrong?*

Your technical skills matter. But what shapes your day-to-day success and your long-term growth is how well you navigate workplace dynamics. These aren't just the obvious things, such as meeting deadlines or contributing in standups. It's the unspoken stuff: how people communicate, how decisions are made, how leadership works, and how responsibility gets handed off (or doesn't).

If this is your first work experience, it might feel like you're walking into a game with no rulebook. Even if you've already been in a few roles, you've probably noticed that every team seems to play by slightly different rules—and no one tells you when they change.

That's what this chapter is here for.

Before we break down generational communication styles, let's set the stage with a skill every high-impact professional shares: reading the room. Understanding how your team functions, on the surface and behind the scenes, will help you avoid misunderstandings, build trust faster, and collaborate with confidence.

> "I think, team first. It allows me to succeed, and it allows my team to succeed."
> —LeBron James, NBA champion and philanthropist

Why team dynamics matter now

Team dynamics aren't just "team vibes" or who gets along with whom. They're the invisible patterns that shape how people collaborate, communicate, make decisions, and respond to change.

And right now? Those patterns are changing fast.

The rise of hybrid and remote work means teams often span time zones, cultures, and platforms. You might go a full project without ever meeting a teammate face-to-face. That shift means old-school trust-building, like hallway chats or Friday drinks, is no longer a given. You have to build a connection with intention.

Then there's AI integration. It's not just that you're using AI-powered tools—your AI teammate might be helping manage timelines, reviewing your work, or suggesting improvements. The way teams operate is no longer human-only. That means being clear about what you need (and when) matters more than ever.

Add generational diversity to the mix, and things get even more layered. In many teams, you're working alongside Millennials, Gen X, and Baby Boomers—each with their own rhythms, communication habits, and work philosophies. It's easy for things to get lost in translation if you're not tuned in.

So what does this mean for you, as a Gen Z professional?

Gen Z has some real advantages. Many are digitally fluent. It's likely you know how to move through tools, messages, and platforms like second nature. You may prefer flexibility and purpose, which can make you a great cultural bridge between rigid systems and a more human-centered future of work.

But if you overlook team dynamics—how others prefer to work, what they need to feel seen, and how decisions actually get made—you risk being misunderstood, left out of key conversations, or seen as "disengaged" when really, you're just working differently.

Mastering team dynamics means knowing how to flex—when to step in, when to ask, when to clarify. And when you do that? You don't just "fit in"—you lead with influence, even if you're early in your work life.

Let's explore what that looks like in action.

Wait, so what are the rules here?

Every workplace has two layers: the official way of doing things and the real way things get done. You might be told everything runs on Slack, but then quickly realize decisions are made in quick calls or private chats. Or you're told, "We work async," but still feel pressure to respond instantly to messages after hours.

That's the unspoken layer—where assumptions live, where frustration builds, and where Gen Z often feels stuck. According to *The Gen Z at Work Study*, Gen Z has a lower tolerance for ambiguity than earlier generations, which means unclear expectations can create unnecessary stress or second-guessing.

One way to adapt? Keep a running "team playbook" note for yourself. Jot down informal norms like who responds quickly, which channels get used for what, and how decisions tend to happen. You'll start spotting patterns fast—and avoid missteps that no one thinks to explain.

Some teams are highly assertive, where feedback is direct and actions move quickly. Others are more consensus-driven or tolerant, where ideas flow gently and feedback is indirect. Neither is better. But if you're tuned into these cues, you'll communicate in a way your team hears.

Who's in charge (and how do they decide)?

Titles don't always reflect who holds influence. In some teams, decisions flow top-down. In others, they're made through direct conversations between team members or relationships. If you're on a power-driven team, structure and hierarchy matter most. In an affiliation-led group, trust and relationships shape choices. In achievement-focused cultures, performance speaks louder than anything else.

This might sound subtle, but it shapes things like who gets listened to and how fast projects move. Don't just look at org charts—watch who people defer to, who gets looped in, and how ideas become decisions.

o-o-o-o-o-o-o-o

Then match your approach. If it is title-led, be sure to go to the person above you and never go around them. If it's a relationship-driven team, build trust before pitching. If it's results-driven, show outcomes. The more attuned you are, the easier it gets to gain support and make your voice heard.

What does taking ownership look like?

Here's one of the trickiest early work-life questions: *When am I supposed to just do it, and when should I check first?*

Some teams operate on sole responsibility: you're assigned something and expected to run with it. Others lean toward shared responsibility, where jumping in to help is expected, even if no one asks. Both can work, but they need different instincts.

If you're unsure, clarify expectations early. Before jumping in, try a message like: "Happy to take the lead on this. Should I fully own it, or would you prefer to co-work together?" That one line signals initiative *and* respect for how your team works.

When roles are vague, silence doesn't always mean "go for it". On the flip side, hesitating too long can make you look checked out. A quick check-in upfront keeps everyone aligned and helps your actions land well.

Decoding generational differences: How each group communicates

By now, you've seen how team dynamics aren't just about what gets done, but *how* it gets done. A big part of that is understanding who's on your team, and how they naturally communicate, collaborate, and make decisions.

This matters more than ever. Teams today might include three or even four generations. And while shared goals bring people together, the way each generation expresses itself, builds trust, and expects feedback can vary wildly. If you're not tuned into those differences, it's easy to feel misunderstood—or worse, to unintentionally offend someone without knowing why.

Let's take a look at who's in the room—and how they work.

Baby Boomers (Born 1946–1964)

Many Baby Boomers today are in executive, senior leadership, or board roles. They've spent decades shaping company cultures, and their influence often carries significant weight in decision-making.

Baby Boomers built their work lives around real-time communication—face-to-face meetings, phone calls, and structured updates. These interactions still represent trust, clarity, and professionalism for them. While most have adapted to digital tools, they still place the highest value on in-person conversations.

If you need their buy-in, don't rely solely on a Slack ping or passive email. Set up a meeting, come prepared with clear bullet points and supporting materials, and follow up with a written summary. Many Baby Boomers appreciate visuals, charts, graphs, and printed docs and will respect you more for showing that level of prep.

> "A quick five-minute call can save us an entire thread of misunderstandings."
> —**Mei, 62, enterprise operations executive**

Gen X (Born 1965–1980)

Gen Xers are often your managers, senior team leads, or independent contributors who oversee complex projects. Gen Xers are direct, independent, and efficiency-driven. They grew up in a work culture where figuring things out on their own was expected. Long-winded explanations? Not their thing. They prefer big-picture strategy over excessive details and trust those who can get straight to the point. If you need a response from a Gen Xer, don't bury your request in a lengthy email. Get to the point fast.

Instead of sending a long-winded explanation about a project issue, try a short message: "Hey, quick input needed. Should we go with Option A (faster, cheaper) or B (higher quality, longer timeline)?" Chances are, they'll respond in under a minute. Decision made. Problem solved.

Gen X also prefers autonomy, so if you ask for guidance, be clear that you've already thought things through. A simple "Here's what I suggest. Do you agree?" can go a long way.

> "If it takes me longer than 30 seconds to figure out what you need, I'm already over it."
> —Raj, 48, creative director

Millennials (Born 1981–1996)

Millennials now make up a large portion of middle management and are often team leads or cross-functional collaborators. They grew up in digital environments and value inclusive leadership.

Unlike Gen X, which leans toward autonomy, many Millennials thrive on collaboration and shared problem-solving. If you drop a fully polished plan on their desk and say, "Let me know what you think," it might feel too closed. Instead, invite them in early: "I've pulled together a rough draft. Want to help me refine it?"

Millennials are fluent in Slack threads, Google Docs, co-editing sessions, and iterative thinking. Don't be surprised if feedback happens in rounds, as collaboration is part of their process. They also value transparency. Be honest about where you're stuck or unsure. A simple, "I'd love your input on this. Here's where I'm hesitating," opens the door to support.

> "Don't just tell me what to do, show me how it connects to the bigger picture, and let's make it better together."
> —Lina, 35, marketing manager

Gen Z (Born 1997–2012)

Gen Z teammates range from interns and associates all the way to managers and founders. Many are also freelancers or side hustlers, balancing multiple projects across platforms.

Compared to earlier generations, many Gen Zers prefer written communication over verbal exchanges. A short Slack message feels efficient: no room for misinterpretation, no wasted time, and a trackable record of decisions. But here's where tension can surface: what feels respectful and clear to Gen Z can seem cold or passive to others.

In fact, *The Gen Z at Work Study* found that Gen Z has a 47% higher preference for written communication compared to earlier generations. So if you've ever been confused by a manager insisting on a "quick meeting to clarify," you're not imagining it—they likely interpret silence or Slack updates as disengagement.

Many Gen Zers also prefer structure and clarity to help them do their best work. Vague requests or abstract feedback can feel disorienting. At the same time, Gen Z tends to rely more on external feedback for confidence, not because they lack ability, but because they're used to fast, affirming responses from digital platforms.

If this sounds like you, it helps to be upfront. Instead of saying, "Let me know what you think," try: "Can you review this by tomorrow? I want to make sure I'm aligned." It's a small shift, but it reduces confusion and shows initiative without waiting for permission.

When working with older teammates, consider flipping your usual order. Start with a big-picture summary, then move into the details. That structure makes your thinking easier to follow and helps bridge the communication gap across generations.

When communication styles clash: Why generational differences cause workplace friction

Even when intentions are good, communication across generations can misfire. A message that feels clear and respectful to you might land as abrupt, confusing, or even passive to someone else, especially if they interpret tone and timing differently.

Many Gen Z teammates prefer to communicate in writing. Slack updates, Notion docs, or task comments feel efficient and avoid confusion. But for earlier generations, especially Gen X and Baby Boomers, that style can sometimes feel too impersonal. They may expect verbal check-ins to build trust or align on the big picture.

This disconnect is about mismatched expectations. And unless you spot the gap early, it can snowball into unnecessary tension.

Jake found this out the hard way. After submitting a project update via Slack, he assumed his Gen X manager would respond in Google Docs. But days later, she scheduled a meeting, frustrated he hadn't followed up.

> "She thought I was ignoring her when, in my mind, I was just waiting for written feedback. She expected an in-person discussion—something I hadn't even considered."
> —Jake, 24, solutions engineer

After that, Jake started asking a simple question upfront: "How do you prefer to give feedback?" That one shift smoothed out misunderstandings before they could escalate and helped his team move faster, with less friction.

That's the heart of this chapter. Navigating workplace dynamics doesn't mean overthinking every message. It just means pausing to notice *how* others prefer to work and flexing your approach when it counts.

The art of workplace influence: How to get people on board (even when they think differently)

Influence at work isn't about being loud, persuasive, or perfect. It's about meeting people where they are and understanding what makes them say yes, what earns their trust, and how they like to process ideas.

You might have a great proposal or a smart solution, but if the way you present it doesn't match your audience's style, it can fall flat. Not because it wasn't a good idea, but because it didn't *land*.

Here's how to flex your communication style in real-world scenarios, based on how different generations and personalities tend to make decisions.

Scenario 1: You need buy-in for a new idea

You've come up with a brilliant solution to improve efficiency in your team, but how do you frame it to get decision-makers on board?

- **Baby Boomers and Gen X:** Lead with credibility and structure. Don't just present an idea, show them why it works with clear reasoning, relevant examples, and the bigger picture. Baby Boomers might appreciate a well-prepared, in-person discussion, while Gen X may want a concise, no-fluff breakdown they can quickly evaluate.

- **Millennials and Gen Z:** Engage them early in the process. Millennials may want to co-create, so bring them into the brainstorming stage before presenting a finished proposal. Gen Z might value efficiency, so get to the point quickly and back it up with data.

Scenario 2: You're facing resistance to change

Maybe you're introducing a new tool, updating a process, or shifting priorities, and not everyone is on board. Here's how to navigate it:

- **Baby Boomers and Gen X:** Resistance from these groups is often about risk and credibility. They need time to evaluate the long-term impact before embracing change. Show them how the new approach aligns with business goals and why it's worth the shift.

- **Millennials and Gen Z:** Resistance here is usually about lack of involvement rather than skepticism. If they feel like a decision was made without their input, they're more likely to push back. Bring them into the conversation early, ask for their perspective, and make them part of the solution.

Scenario 3: You're struggling to get noticed

You're doing great work, but it's not being recognized. Here's how to make an impact:

- **Baby Boomers and Gen X:** Be proactive about visibility. Don't assume they'll notice your contributions; make sure your work is seen. Share updates strategically (without oversharing) and focus on outcomes, not effort.

- **Millennials and Gen Z:** These groups may be more vocal about recognition, so engage them in mutual support. If you amplify their wins, they'll likely do the same for you. Be visible in collaborative spaces like Slack, meetings, and project discussions.

When you understand the "recipes" each generation needs, you stop feeling frustrated by communication gaps and start navigating workplace dynamics like a pro. That's when you stop second-guessing yourself. That's when your ideas start landing. And that's when your work life begins to accelerate in ways you never imagined.

Cracking the communication code: How different generations prefer to connect

Each generation approaches work through a different motivational lens, shaped by their experiences and preferences. Recognizing these underlying drivers can help you tailor your communication style and reduce friction when working across age groups.

Baby Boomers: Goal-driven and relationship-centered communicators

If you've ever pitched an idea to a Baby Boomer and felt like they needed more convincing, it's probably because you skipped a key step: building the relationship first. Unlike Gen X, who prefer efficiency, or Millennials, who likely thrive on back-and-forth collaboration, Baby Boomers place just as much emphasis on who they're working with as they do on what's being discussed.

> "I don't just approve ideas; I invest in the people behind them."
> —David, 64, venture partner, private equity firm

So, before jumping into business, take a moment to connect. A quick "Hope you had a great weekend!" or "Looking forward to catching up" might seem small, but for Baby Boomers, this kind of personal touch builds trust. Once you have that, you'll find they're much more open to supporting your ideas. And when you do present your thoughts, keep them structured and goal-focused—they want to see a clear connection between your idea and the bigger picture.

If you want their buy-in, as we've mentioned, don't just rely on Slack messages or a quick email. This generation thrives in visual environments—they're drawn to face-to-face conversations, printed documents, detailed reports, and visual tools like graphs and charts. If you want to earn a Baby Boomer's trust, show up in person when you can, and bring clear visuals to back up your ideas. Follow up with a summary, and show them that you respect their experience and value their input, not just their approval.

Gen X: Independent thinkers who value accountability and connection

For Gen X, actions speak louder than words, especially when it comes to communication. They've built their work identity on autonomy, credibility, and practical results. While they collaborate well in teams, they likely value clearly defined individual ownership and don't need constant validation to feel secure in their decisions.

What makes Gen Xers tick is trust through competency. They're less interested in being looped into every little update. If something's going off track? Yes, they may want to know. But otherwise, they may want to see that you've got it handled.

So, how do you build trust with Gen X teammates or managers?

- Keep your communication short, sharp, and section-focused.
- Instead of saying, "I'm stuck on this," try, "Here's the challenge, and here's what I've done so far. Does this direction make sense?"
- Respect their time by skipping the details.

> "I don't need to be updated on every step, but I do want to know what decisions you're making and why. That's how I know you're thinking it through."
> —Darren, 46, team lead in enterprise tech

They may seem hands-off, but they're paying attention. When they see you taking ownership and moving things forward independently, you'll gain their trust faster, and their respect will follow.

Millennials: Recognition-driven and impact-focused communicators

Millennials aren't just collaborative, they're more likely to be driven by impact. If they're going to invest time in something, they might want to know why it matters and how their input will make a difference. That means if you want their support, bring them into the conversation early.

Instead of saying, "Here's what I need you to do," try framing it as a shared opportunity: "I've started mapping this out, but I'd love your input on how we can make it better." That shift from instruction to collaboration makes all the difference. And when you're asking for their feedback, be transparent. Millennials prefer honest, open conversations, so don't be afraid to say, "Here's what I'm struggling with. What do you think?"

> "I don't just want to be told what to do. I want to understand why it matters and how we can make it even better as a team."
> —Tasha, 36, customer experience lead

When a Millennial gives input, acknowledge it. They may thrive on recognition, so even a quick "Great idea, I'll incorporate that" makes them feel valued and keeps them engaged in the process.

Gen Z: Detail-oriented realists who thrive on clarity

As a Gen Zer, you likely prefer direct, structured communication, clear steps, straight answers, and no wasted time. That's why long, meandering meetings may feel frustrating, and why waiting days for feedback may make you question whether your work is even being reviewed.

Unlike earlier generations, Gen Z is likely to be highly reliant on external feedback. You might seek validation, not because you lack ideas, but because you might want to make sure you're on the right path. You prefer structured collaboration and may need context to perform at your best. When communication gets too abstract or ambiguous, it's easy to feel overwhelmed or disengaged.

But things can get tricky: earlier generations don't always move at your speed. If you send a Slack message and don't get a response right away, it doesn't mean they're ignoring you. It might just mean they process information differently. So, if you need feedback, be upfront about it. Instead of saying, "Let me know your thoughts," try, "Can you review this by tomorrow?" Setting expectations helps avoid frustration on both sides.

> "If I don't get feedback quickly, I assume something is wrong, or worse, that it's been ignored."
> —Aaliyah, 25, content strategist

And when someone asks you for a "high-level strategy", resist the urge to go straight into the details. Earlier generations often think in broad strokes first, so start with a quick summary, then break it down step by step. It helps them see the big picture before diving into specifics and makes your communication even more effective.

> "Influence isn't about age or experience. It's about understanding what makes people tick. When you get to know how others prefer to work, you become the person they trust, follow, and want on their team." —Dan Negroni

Mastering remote and global teams: Avoiding the burnout trap

As the Workverse becomes more global and remote, mastering cross-cultural collaboration is just as important as managing generational dynamics. Working across time zones means that instant responses aren't always realistic, and communication needs to be more intentional.

Omar, a Gen Z engineer working with a distributed team spanning the US, Australia, and the UK, found himself constantly responding to messages at odd hours, feeling pressure to always be online. The fix? He and his team agreed on core overlap hours for real-time meetings and set clear expectations for asynchronous communication. They used scheduling tools to avoid unnecessary late-night messages and established clear guidelines for when responses were needed.

If you're working with colleagues across time zones, take the lead in clarifying expectations. Set response-time norms, be mindful of cultural differences in communication styles, and avoid burnout by establishing boundaries for when you're available.

Build a team that clicks

Navigating workplace dynamics can feel overwhelming, especially when stepping into new environments, forming fresh teams, or managing unspoken norms. Each teammate brings their own communication style, decision-making process, and generational expectations. This exercise will help you become the kind of collaborator who can connect across any team by understanding what truly motivates the people around you and how to meet them where they are.

Step 1: Map your generational mix

Think about the people you work with most often. What generations do they represent—Baby Boomers? Gen X? Millennials? Your fellow Gen Zs? Jot them down.

_____

_____

_____

_____

Step 2: Compare yourself to each generation

 Log in to Marlee.com and head to *Boards*.

Each Board shows you where your work style lines up with theirs, and where it doesn't. It's like having a cheat sheet for collaboration. You'll know when teamwork will flow naturally, and importantly, how to bridge the gap when misunderstandings might pop up.

Create a Board for each generation you work with:

- *Gen Z and Me*
- *Millennials and Me*
- *Gen X and Me*
- *Baby Boomers and Me*

Take note of your similarities and differences

_____

_____

_____

_____

Step 3: Dive into one-to-one dynamics

Want to work better with a specific teammate or manager? Use Marlee's 1 to 1 comparison Board. In seconds, you'll get tailored insights, almost like shortcuts, for how to connect faster, avoid unnecessary friction, and make your message land.

See your top motivators side by side, then *Ask Marlee*:

- "How do I work best with @teammate?"
- "How can I avoid conflict with @teammate?"
- "How do I convince @teammate?"

Jot the insights that shift your approach

_____

_____

Step 4: Host a team dynamics workshop

Starting on a new team? Or leading one? Create a Team Space in the Marlee app and invite your teammates to join. Then create a 1 to *Many* Board and a *Team Distribution* Board to see how your group's motivations are distributed.

Use this as the foundation for a short workshop to give your team a live mirror of how you work together. You can:

- Uncover which communication styles work best (Slack vs. calls? Structured docs vs. spontaneous chats?).
- Spot team strengths and blind spots.
- Set shared norms that make collaboration smoother.

This isn't just a one-time activity; it's a culture builder. When everyone understands how each other ticks, the work gets better (and way more fun).

Review your 1 to Many Board and identify key insights for the workshop

___

___

___

"You don't have to change who you are to thrive on a team. But if you can flex your approach just a little, that's where real influence begins."
—Coach Marlee

Step 5: Your weekly challenge

What's one small shift you'll make this week to navigate your team dynamics more effectively? Maybe it's tweaking how you ask for feedback, clarifying expectations earlier, or adjusting how you present ideas to someone from another generation.

Pick one. Try it out. Then check in with yourself—how did it go?

___

___

___

"The fastest way to reduce friction at work is through curiosity. When you lead with curiosity about how others operate, you turn tension into trust, and collaboration gets easier."
—Michelle Duval

Make generational differences and team dynamics your superpower

You've just unlocked one of the most underrated workplace skills: learning how to flex your communication and collaboration style across generations. You've also started to tune into the deeper layers of team dynamics—the unspoken rules, decision-making styles, and responsibility handoffs that shape how work gets done.

Now you know what motivates each generation, how they prefer to connect, and how to spot friction before it snowballs. You're starting to see that influence comes from knowing how to speak in a way that resonates.

When you can adapt without losing yourself, ask the right questions, and read the room before reacting—that's when people start to see you as someone they trust, follow, and want on their team.

Up next: You'll learn how to stop grinding and start flowing by aligning your daily tasks with what genuinely energizes you. Because high performance comes from working with your motivation, not against it.

Part 3
Unlock Your Peak Potential

Now that you've mapped your Workverse, it's time to unlock your full power. In this part, we'll show you how to stay energized, lead with confidence, and work smarter with the help of AI teammates, so you can grow faster without burning out.

CHAPTER 12

Mastering Your Flow

TL;DR

You're not lazy. You're likely just out of alignment. Fix that, and everything shifts.

This chapter explains the real cause of Gen Z burnout—not overwork but working *against* your natural motivators. Flow is your antidote. When you match your work to what energizes you, everything from focus to fulfillment improves.

- **Burnout:** a mismatch between how you work and how you're wired.

- **Flow:** the sweet spot where your skills and challenges align. You're focused, creative, and fulfilled.

- **Gen Z tends to thrive on clarity, feedback, structure, and purpose:** a lack of these = mental drain.

- **Motivational alignment fuels energy:** it's not about doing less; it's about doing what fits.

- **Redesign your week around what energizes you:** protect your flow state, task by task.

The real reason you're burning out

What if burnout isn't just about too much work, but the wrong kind of work? Fifty-four percent of Gen Z and younger Millennials report feeling stressed a lot of the time.[34]

Burnout isn't just about being tired. It's chronic stress that leads to mental exhaustion, disengagement, and declining well-being. And Gen Z is more vulnerable to burnout than any other generation.

Why? Because energy drains happen when work misaligns with motivation. *The Gen Z at Work Study* found that your generation works very differently from the earlier generations.

While previous generations tend to be energized by big-picture thinking, long-term vision-setting, and abstract strategy, you're more likely to be motivated by solving real-world problems, working in detail, and receiving frequent, practical feedback.

And when you're forced into older styles of working that don't match those motivators—like distant goals, ambiguous expectations, or rigid bureaucratic systems—your energy drains fast. The result? Skyrocketing levels of burnout, anxiety, and disconnection.

Energy comes from motivational alignment

We often treat burnout like it's just about workload. But you could work long hours on something you love and feel completely alive. Burnout happens when there's a mismatch—when the way you're being asked to work goes against how you naturally work best. It's like swimming against the current all day. You might get there, but you'll be exhausted.

> "Burnout is a warning signal. It's your body and mind telling you something's off. When we listen and lean into what motivates us, we don't just prevent burnout, we unlock work that energizes, excites, and fulfills us." —**Michelle Duval**

So what's the alternative to grinding through misaligned tasks? That's where flow theory comes in. Psychologist Mihaly Csikszentmihalyi coined the term *flow* to describe a state of deep focus where you're so engaged in a task that everything else fades away.

Time distorts, so much so that you might feel like hours pass in what feels like minutes. You lose self-consciousness. You're not thinking about whether you're doing a good job; you just are. Work feels effortless and intrinsically rewarding. You're not chasing an outcome; you're immersed in the experience itself.

Think about the last time you were editing a video, coding a project, sketching, or even getting lost in a long strategy game. You weren't checking the clock—you were in it. That's flow.

> "Enjoyment appears at the boundary between boredom and anxiety, when the challenges are just balanced with the person's capacity to act."
> —**Mihaly Csikszentmihalyi, psychologist**

Flow happens when your skills are perfectly matched to the level of challenge. Not so easy that you get bored. Not so hard that you freeze up in anxiety. But right in that sweet spot where your attention is fully engaged. You know what needs to happen next, and each step naturally flows into the next. You feel in control, yet free.

When you experience flow regularly, work becomes energizing and wonderfully joyful. You perform better, you feel more creative, and you're less likely to burn out. It's not just a nice-to-have. It's one of the most powerful states for building a fulfilling and sustainable work life.

Your motivations are the gateway to flow

Flow might look like magic from the outside, but it's not random, and it's not the same for everyone. That deep state of focus? It starts with knowing how you're wired to work.

Motivations are your inner compass for how you approach work. Some of us come alive when collaborating with a team, bouncing ideas around in real time. Others feel at their best when working independently, free to think deeply and set their own pace. Some of us thrive in clear structure and step-by-step plans, while others feel energized by flexibility and exploring different ways to solve a problem. Some people prefer to reflect, observe, and think things through before jumping in. Others get their spark from diving straight into action and figuring things out as they go.

These patterns are measurable, stable preferences that shape how you engage with tasks, teams, decisions, and environments. At Marlee, we call them motivational traits. When your work life matches these preferences, everything flows more naturally. Your brain isn't wasting energy resisting the way you're working—it's focused, engaged, and fueled.

Now here's where flow theory and motivation science meet. Mihaly Csikszentmihalyi identified key conditions for flow: clear goals, immediate feedback, a sense of control, and that perfect balance between challenge and skill. But whether those conditions *feel right* for you depends on your motivations.

If you're someone who needs time to reflect before making a decision, constant pressure to act fast can throw you off. If you're wired to prefer collaboration, but you're isolated all day, the work may never feel rewarding, no matter how skilled you are. If you crave structure and clarity, but your environment is chaotic and ambiguous, it's going to feel like trying to build a puzzle without the picture.

Flow can't be forced. But it can be *designed*. It starts by understanding what motivates you and shaping your work around those traits.

Flow is also deeply personal. One person finds it in a solo coding sprint. Another gets there while leading a brainstorming session with a dozen teammates. Someone else might find it solving problems behind the scenes, noticing the small details no one else sees. The key isn't copying someone else's path. It's identifying *your* path to deep engagement.

Motivational science backs this up. When your work activates your natural preferences, your brain releases dopamine. That's the same chemical linked to focus, reward, and learning. In other words, when your motivations are in play, effort feels easier. Your attention sharpens. Your curiosity wakes up. You don't need to *try* to concentrate—your brain's already hooked.

That's the power of motivational alignment. It creates the ideal conditions for flow to emerge and makes it repeatable.

In the next section, we'll explore what happens when this alignment breaks down. Because once you know what flow feels like, you'll also know exactly what it feels like when it's missing.

Let's look at what happens when you're out of alignment

You can push through work that doesn't fit you for a while. But if most of your workdays are filled with tasks that pull you out of your natural rhythm, it's draining on a deep level.

Motivation science shows that when your work life is aligned with your core drivers—what truly energizes you—you perform better, recover faster, and feel more fulfilled. Ideally, about 80% of your week should be aligned with your natural motivations. That doesn't mean every moment needs to be perfect. You can absolutely handle a few tasks that push you outside your preferences. But when misalignment becomes the norm, that's when stress builds up, motivation dips, and burnout becomes inevitable.

And there's another layer here: *meaning*. One of the most powerful predictors of motivation and well-being at work is whether or not your work feels meaningful.

> "One cannot lead a life that is truly excellent without feeling that one belongs to something greater and more permanent than oneself."
> —Mihaly Csikszentmihalyi, psychologist

Flow happens most easily when the task feels meaningful on its own—when you're not forcing it, you're immersed in it.

> "Working hard for something we don't care about is called stress. Working hard for something we love is called passion."
> —Simon Sinek, leadership expert and author

And psychologist, Adam Grant, adds:

> "The most meaningful way to succeed is to help others succeed."
> —Adam Grant, organizational psychologist

Whether it's contributing to a mission you believe in, building something you're proud of, or simply solving real problems for real people, meaningful work doesn't just feel good—it makes you more resilient, more focused, and more creative. When your work has purpose, you're more likely to show up energized, even when the pressure's high.

But without that connection to purpose, your energy becomes fragmented. Disengagement creeps in. You start questioning why you're doing what you're doing in the first place.

So if you're feeling off, it's not just about the tasks on your to-do list. It could be a signal that your work is out of sync with what motivates you and what matters most to you. And if that misalignment continues unchecked? That's when we start to see the early signs of something deeper: burnout.

What science says about burnout

We're not just talking about feeling a little tired or needing a day off. Burnout is a physiological and psychological response to prolonged misalignment, and 40% of Gen Z reports feeling stressed "all or most of the time."[25] The World Health Organization has classified burnout as a workplace syndrome. And research shows that younger workers are experiencing cognitive overload and emotional disengagement at record levels.[35]

Burnout isn't just emotional, it's physical. Chronic stress affects your sleep, weakens your immune system, and impairs memory and decision-making. When you're working against your natural motivations day after day, the physiological toll adds up.

Tasks that require heavy cognitive switching, ambiguous instructions, or long periods without feedback can be especially draining for Gen Z. And when your energy isn't replenished, motivation and well-being quickly collapse.

So, what's the real solution? The answer isn't just about managing stress alone; it's about creating a resilience system that helps you protect your energy before burnout takes over. The goal isn't just to survive work. It's to thrive in a way that feels sustainable, fulfilling, and energizing. Let's dive into how you can make that happen.

Why Gen Z is burning out faster than other generations

If you're constantly pushing through tasks that drain you without recovery or re-alignment, you may be on a fast track to burnout. Let's break down the six most common energy drains for Gen Z, according to *The Gen Z at Work Study*, and explore how to reframe each.

Long-term targets feel like an energy drain

It's unlikely that you're lazy. You just need to see progress now, not years from now. Earlier work structures are built around climbing the ladder, waiting years for promotions, and working toward five-year plans. But for Gen Z, long-term goals with distant rewards often feel like running on a treadmill with no finish line.

You need to see progress, not just hear vague promises about "paying your dues." You tend to thrive on short feedback loops and visible wins.

> "I was stuck in a job where everything was about hitting long-term KPIs that felt totally disconnected from my day-to-day work. I needed wins I could actually see."
> —Mika, 24, data analyst

If your work revolves around long-term targets without tangible, short-term milestones, burnout isn't just possible, it's inevitable.

Make progress visible, even in the small stuff

Think about your current role. Are you seeing clear progress in what you do? If you're finding you are not able to recognize progress, set aside time each week in your calendar to answer the following questions: *What problems have I solved in the last week?* and *What are the small wins I achieved this week?* The key to answering both of these questions is to look for the small problems, not just the big ones. Over time, they all add up to a larger problem.

Waiting for feedback feels like walking in the dark

Gen Z is highly motivated to seek external references for research and feedback when making decisions. *The Gen Z at Work Study* found a 56% increase in this preference compared to earlier generations. Without feedback, you might not just feel unsure of how you're doing—you could also be drained by the mental load of second-guessing. Imagine walking into a room with no lights, no windows, and no idea where you're supposed to go. That's what it feels like when you don't get feedback at work. Gen Z is more likely to thrive with clear, immediate feedback, but many workplaces still operate on outdated models where you hear how you're doing once a year in a formal review.

If you're constantly second-guessing yourself or feeling like you're working in isolation, it's a warning sign for potential burnout. A lack of feedback can drain your confidence, leaving you feeling more exhausted than you should be.

"I used to think burnout was just about being tired, but it's way more than that. It's feeling like no matter how much effort you put in, it doesn't actually lead anywhere. After months of overworking in a role with no clear direction, I realized it wasn't just exhaustion; I had lost all motivation to even try."
—Jordan, 26, account manager

Seek frequent feedback to stay energized

Reflect on your last project. Did you ask for feedback that helped you improve and stay motivated? Or were you left wondering if your work even made an impact?

"What's one way you could build a feedback loop into your next project? Feedback fuels clarity and clarity protects your energy."
—Coach Marlee

Since external validation might be a key motivator, make sure you have a regular feedback loop in place. If your workplace doesn't naturally offer one, be proactive, schedule regular check-ins with your manager, or ask for feedback after key projects, such as a team retrospective. Knowing you're on track prevents second-guessing from draining your mental energy.

Big-picture thinking feels overwhelming without clear steps

Overall, Gen Z is found to prefer detail over ambiguity. Being dropped into abstract, high-level planning without structure can feel paralyzing, like landing in a foreign city with no GPS. If that's your daily work experience, it's no surprise you feel drained. Your brain wants a roadmap, not a vague destination.

High-level strategic planning, "blue-sky thinking," and open-ended brainstorming might sound great to some, but for many Gen Zers, these tasks lead to mental overload. Abstract strategy talks? Not energizing, unless someone connects them to practical action. You tend to work best when given clear steps, structured plans, and well-defined expectations.

Are you being asked to "figure things out" without enough detail? How often do you feel like you're expected to connect the dots without enough information? If you find situations like this stressful or draining, give yourself permission to ask more questions of your team or an AI teammate to gain the level of detail or information you need to feel confident in the task at hand.

Prioritize step-by-step work over big-picture ambiguity

If high-level strategy conversations leave you feeling lost, focus on roles and tasks that offer clear, structured steps. Project management tools, checklists, and well-defined processes can help make large goals feel more achievable and reduce mental fatigue.

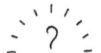

"If strategy meetings leave you overwhelmed, ask yourself *What's the first small action I can take?* Process turns fog into forward motion."
—Coach Marlee

Rigid workplace rules feel suffocating

You're not anti-structure; you just want the freedom to question outdated systems and suggest better ones. Rigid bureaucracy is a fast track to disengagement. Gen Z is known for ignoring bureaucracy, and for good reason. You likely prefer flexibility over rigid policies. If you're stuck in an organization that enforces outdated, inefficient systems or micromanages every small decision, your motivation could plummet. It's frustrating, and over time, feeling trapped in a structure that doesn't allow for adaptability fuels burnout.

Find flexibility in your work environment

Does your work environment give you the flexibility to operate in a way that suits your strengths? If not, where are the constraints that drain your energy? Identify an alternative that would better support and bring out the best in you. Identify who in your team you can approach to make your request.

If rigid rules and excessive processes drain you, look for workplaces that prioritize autonomy and adaptability. Set boundaries with micromanagers, negotiate flexible work terms, or, if needed, shift toward roles that value results over adherence to unnecessary protocols.

> "Where do you need more flexibility? Choose one area where the rules feel stifling and explore how you can co-create a better way with your team."
> —Coach Marlee

Meetings, calls, and verbal instructions are exhausting

Most Gen Zers process information better in writing. Endless meetings and spoken instructions—especially without a clear purpose—don't energize you; they can overwhelm you. *The Gen Z at Work Study* found that Gen Z prefers written communication over verbal communication. That means if your job requires constant phone calls, live presentations, or brainstorming discussions, you may feel mentally exhausted faster than colleagues who thrive in those settings.

> "I negotiated a hybrid schedule with fewer meetings and started using project management software. Within months, I felt re-energized."
> —Sienna, 24, project coordinator

Balance meetings and verbal communication with more written workflows

Do you get more clarity from written instructions than verbal ones? If you do, explore using AI tools such as Fathom to transcribe meetings into written notes. Or use whiteboards and other tools to take your own written notes to help you stay focused during meetings. You can also invite and ask for written documentation, asynchronous updates, and structured written feedback from teammates.

> "If meetings drain you, ask for agendas in advance, take written notes during, and follow up in writing. It helps your brain stay focused and your energy stay protected."
> —Coach Marlee

High-pressure decision-making can feel paralyzing

Snap decisions aren't always Gen Z's style. You may prefer to gather input before choosing. When pushed to act too fast, your motivation can crash. Unlike previous generations, who prefer to make snap decisions, Gen Z prefers pausing, reflecting, and gathering more input before acting. You often look to others before trusting your gut. In high-pressure situations, without support, decision-making can feel overwhelming. These aren't flaws. They're motivational mismatches. And when left unchecked, they can, over time, lead to burnout.

Give yourself the time you need to decide with confidence

If you're thrown into high-pressure situations where you need to make rapid choices without time to think, stress levels can skyrocket. If this sounds like you, it is not always a lack of confidence—it's most often just not how your energy flows best.

Do you feel rushed when making decisions at work? If so, you're not alone. Many Gen Zers need time and clarity before they feel confident enough to act. Start by identifying how many exposures—or rounds of input—you typically need before you're ready to make a decision. Then communicate that to your team. It's not about hesitating—it's about aligning your decision-making with how you work best. When your process is supported, your confidence and energy grow.

> "Start by noticing your natural decision-making rhythm. Do you need to research first? Talk it through? Try it out? Whatever your process is, own it. Before your next decision, give yourself a confidence boost by asking for input or breaking it into smaller steps. Then tell your team what you need to decide well. You're not slow—you're thoughtful. Let's turn that into a strength."
> —Coach Marlee

This is why the hustle may still feel empty

By now, you've probably seen some of your own work patterns reflected in those energy drains. But burnout isn't just about having too much on your plate. It's about working in ways that constantly pull you out of alignment.

That's why most burnout advice, like "take a break" or "set boundaries," only scratches the surface. Those things help, but they don't fix the root cause. Because if your tasks keep clashing with your core motivators, your energy will keep leaking out.

That's where motivational alignment comes in. The better your work fits your natural drivers, the easier it becomes to stay focused, perform well, and feel fulfilled. You don't need to overhaul your entire job overnight, but you can start small. You can redesign your work from the inside out.

"The more you are positive and say, 'I want to have a good life,' the more you build that reality for yourself."
—Chris Pine, actor

And that's exactly what we'll walk through next

Realign your work with what energizes you

You've just explored the science behind what energizes you: flow, motivation, and meaning. You've seen how burnout can stem from working in ways that clash with your natural strengths and how fulfillment comes when your work aligns with what matters to you.

But what do you do with that insight?

In earlier chapters, you created your *Individual Results Board* in Marlee. You've looked at what motivates you, how you prefer to work, your unique strengths, and the kind of environment that brings out your best. Now it's time to revisit those insights through a new lens—one shaped by everything you now know about motivational alignment and the science of flow.

So, how do you figure out what gives your work meaning, and design a role that fits you? That's where Marlee can help. Backed by more than 90% reliability, it gives you a clear view of what drives you and how that connects to the way you work best. You'll get personalized insights into the tasks, environments, and daily rhythms that align with your unique motivational makeup.

Whether you're redesigning your current role or exploring what to do next, these insights help you shift your work life, one small change at a time, grounded in what works for you.

"You can't change the system overnight, but you can change how you operate within it. Just start shifting the ratio. Eighty percent of your week should energize you, not exhaust you."
—Dan Negroni

Step 1: Explore your motivations in *My Profile & Results*

Head to the Marlee.com app, log in, and click on your avatar in the top-right corner. From there, open your *My Profile & Results* page. This is your personal hub; it brings together everything you've learned about what energizes you at work.

Start by filtering your motivational traits from highest to lowest. You can toggle between *Bubbles* (for a visual map of your traits) or *Distributions* (for a deeper dive into how each trait compares to the benchmark in your local culture). Either way, you're getting a personalized map of your work energy: your zones of flow, friction, and potential.

Your top 10-20 motivations are the ones that hold the most energy, fulfillment, and interest for you at work.

- Which motivations spark a sense of challenge that feels exciting, not overwhelming?
- Which strengths help you lose track of time in the best way?
- Where do you feel most "in sync" with yourself and others?

"I always knew I liked solving problems, but seeing how it connects to my flow state made me rethink how I spend my mornings. I now block out deep-focus time for strategy work, and it's changed everything."
—Jalen, 23, business operations associate

o o o o

Think about a time you felt truly engaged. What were you doing? Who were you with? Was the task meaningful on its own, or did it serve a bigger purpose? That's your motivational energy showing up in real life.

_____

_____

_____

_____

Step 2: *Ask Marlee* what fuels you

Gain instant insights tailored to your unique motivational makeup.

Marlee won't just tell you what you're motivated by; it'll help you understand what gives you energy, and what pulls you out of flow. You'll uncover the types of tasks, environments, and interactions that help you thrive more consistently.

Click *Ask Marlee* and type:

- "What motivates and brings out the best in me?"

"I realized I thrive on practical impact. So instead of chasing flashy roles, I looked for teams where my work makes a clear difference. That's where I found real motivation."
— **Tanvi, 24, operations**

Write down any surprises. Notice any patterns. These insights are tools to design your next week differently.

_____

_____

_____

_____

Step 3: Audit and redesign part of your week

Look at your calendar and create a document that lists out your current day-to-day, weekly, and monthly tasks—either in your current role or one you're considering.

Copy Marlee's insights into this doc and start a task-by-task audit.

Audit your ideal flow states: to what degree are the tasks aligned with your top motivations (see your *My Profile & Results* page) and the insights from Marlee? Score each one from 0–100%:

- 0% = totally out of sync with your motivations
- 100% = perfectly aligned
- 50% = somewhere in between

Now step back and ask:

- *How well does your current role—or one you're considering—meet these?*
- *Where is there alignment, and where is there friction?*

> "I used to bounce between tasks and felt totally scattered. I set up a Monday routine where I start with a 'thinking hour'—no meetings. It's helped me get ahead instead of constantly reacting."
> **—Enzo, 25, product support**

How much of your week is spent on tasks that energize you? How much is stuck in energy-draining zones? If 80% of your time aligns with your motivations, great, you're on track. But if that balance is reversed, your system's working against you.

Awareness is the first lever of change.

_____

_____

_____

Now, take what you've discovered and rework just one part of your week. You don't have to change everything. Maybe you protect one deep-work hour in the morning. Or maybe you shift a draining solo task into a quick collab session if teamwork fuels you.

_____

_____

_____

_____

"I started time-blocking creative work for the morning and saving meetings for after lunch. Total game changer."
—Zara, 23, brand designer

Step 4: Start energizing weekly rituals

Rituals are your recharging stations. Even tiny ones can reconnect you to meaning and momentum.

Pick one small, energizing ritual and build it into your week.

- A Friday reflection to celebrate what energized you
- A Monday reset to align your week with your top motivations
- A short midweek check-in: *What's giving me energy right now?*

_____

_____

> "When we stop pushing through and start aligning our work to what motivates us, we unlock not just energy, but joy, resilience, and the power to thrive."
> —**Coach Marlee**

Step 5: Align 80% of your week to your motivations

If your week is trending low in alignment with your motivations, use the confidence you gained in Step 4 to start redesigning your week. Adjust your tasks, role, or work environment to better reflect what energizes you—and see what it unleashes within you!

_____

_____

_____

_____

Future proofing your resilience

Resilience isn't about pushing harder—it's about working smarter, in ways that match how you're wired to thrive. It's a skill you build by staying close to your energy and designing work that supports your motivations. Burnout happens when your work life keeps pulling you away from yourself.

But the opposite is also true: thriving has begun for you by using this playbook and continues to start each and every moment you begin working with yourself, not against. Start small. One task, one tweak, one pattern shift. The sooner you start working with your energy, not against it, the sooner you unlock a work life that fuels you.

Up next: We'll show you how to take this energy alignment one step further—by designing a productivity system that fits *you*, your motivation, and your flow.

Create your productivity stack!

CHAPTER 13

Hack Your Productivity

TL;DR

Productivity starts with alignment.

High performance isn't about doing more; it's about decoding what brings out the best in you.

- **Productivity is an energy game:** align 80% of your week to your top motivations, and you'll perform better with less effort.
- **Work with your natural rhythms:** track when your energy peaks, set up daily rituals, and match important tasks to your best focus times.
- **Design your day your way:** solo or team, structure or flexibility—set it up to fit how you operate best.
- **Cut decision clutter:** lean on AI tools, routines, and shortcuts to save focus for what matters.
- **Use your Marlee *Productivity Board*:** spot your strengths, audit your habits, and realign one thing each week.

Let's take you behind the scenes

From tech founders to elite athletes to startup teams—those who perform at the highest levels aren't just time managers. They're energy hackers.

They've learned to design their work life around what energizes them—and minimize what drains them. At the core of their productivity: daily rituals, a deep understanding of what drives them, and next-level outsourcing.

And as you have just learned in Chapter 12, that starts with motivation. When your day is built around your highest motivations—the things that feel meaningful, natural, and energizing—you don't just get more done. You enter into flow. You feel fulfilled. You perform at your best.

That's the heartbeat of Marlee's research. When 80% of your work aligns with your top motivations, and less than 20% falls into the zone that drains you, you don't burn out. You thrive. And when your systems, rituals, and decisions follow that same alignment, your energy becomes your superpower.

But when alignment is off—even if your calendar looks manageable—things can unravel fast.

Research shows the average adult makes tens of thousands of decisions per day—some studies cite as many as 35,000.[36] Most are small decisions. But together, they add up to one powerful cost: decision fatigue.

After coaching thousands of high performers between us, we've seen firsthand that energy isn't just lost in big moments—it leaks through the constant, low-stakes choices we make all day long.

> "One of the greatest hidden costs to performance is decision fatigue. High performers protect their energy by using daily rituals, delegation, and personalized systems to reduce the number of unnecessary choices they make."
> —Michelle Duval

This chapter is your guide to building your own version of that system—one designed around how *you* work best.

Work with your natural rhythms, not against them

Let's start by noticing when your energy peaks and crashes. Do you come alive at 10 am? Or get in the zone late at night? Maybe you're the kind of person who works best in bursts, not marathons.

This is about understanding how *you* operate and building your workflow around it. When you match your most important tasks to your natural energy curve, productivity stops being a grind and becomes your rhythm.

The daily rituals that keep you grounded (and going)

Start and end with intention and with gratitude

Let's talk about rituals. Not the time-consuming kind, just the small, repeatable ones that give your day shape, protect your energy, and set the tone for everything else.

High performers often swear by them. Why? Because your brain doesn't thrive in chaos. It craves anchors: predictable points that help you shift gears and recover between sprints. These are grounding moments that reduce stress, sharpen focus, and help your brain anticipate flow.

Start by asking yourself, *How do I begin and end my day?*

Are you easing in with intention, or rolling straight into the noise? Are you winding down with reflection and gratitude, or doomscrolling until your brain fries?

> "Your morning ritual isn't just for calm, it's a declaration of who you want to be that day."
> —**Shadé Zahrai, co-founder and director of Influenceo Global Inc**

The most effective rituals? They're often the simplest.

One standout tool? Michelle's favorite, and most simple hack, is *The Five Minute Journal*. It prompts you to set your morning intention. *What would make today great?* And close with reflection and gratitude: *What did I learn?* Or *what am I thankful for?*

Those five minutes can make the difference between a reactive day and one that's consciously designed.

If you prefer a digital twist, your AI teammate can ease you in with intentional prompts:

- "Here's what's coming up."
- "You've had a big week—maybe start slower today."
- "Want to focus on creative work before noon?"
- "What's something you're grateful for before you start today?"

Evening rituals work the same way—no need for a complex routine. Just ask yourself:

- *What felt good today?*
- *What do I need more or less of tomorrow?*
- *Would a quiet read or a walk serve me best tonight?*

And if you're not sure where to start? Ask your AI teammate:

- "Can you build me a five-minute ritual with hydration, gratitude, and one energizing prompt?"
- "What's one thing I can do this evening to help me reset?"

Or skip the tech. Just light a candle. Take a breath. Jot a win. The magic isn't in the tool; it's in the consistency of intention setting and reflecting.

The goal is to start and end your day with intention, and to remind your brain what you *want* to focus on, rather than letting the world decide for you.

Align with how you work best

Let's go deeper here. Productivity is about working in a way that fits how *you* naturally operate. You have a unique way of focusing, deciding, starting things, collaborating, and taking in information. When those work rhythms match your top motivations, everything gets easier.

This chapter is about discovering your best ways of working and designing your day around them. That's how high performers do it. They don't force themselves to work in ways that drain them. They build systems that align with their energy.

Think of your daily energy like a budget. You've only got so much to spend. If you're using it up on tasks that clash with your preferences—like collaborating all day when you need quiet solo time, or working in isolation when you get energy from bouncing ideas around—you'll burn through that energy budget before noon.

If 80% of your week aligns with your top ten motivations and less than 20% is spent in your lowest, you're more likely to stay focused, energized, and fulfilled. That's when productivity starts to feel effortless and when your strengths become superpowers.

So what happens when you don't work this way?

When your days are filled with tasks that clash with your lowest motivations, your brain works harder just to stay focused. You might feel foggy, distracted, or constantly behind. Over time, that mismatch can lead to burnout, underperformance, and the quiet frustration of knowing you're capable of more but never quite hitting your stride.

You start to question your abilities when it's not your talent that's the problem, it's the setup. Your ways of working are misaligned.

So let's explore your preferences across key areas: your ideal workspace, how you like to communicate, how you start projects, how you take ownership, how much routine vs. variety you need, and how you make decisions. Once you know these, you'll have the power to hack your productivity and set yourself up to thrive.

Design your day around your ideal workspace

Let's start with where—and how—you work best. Everyone has a unique rhythm, and one of the most important things to figure out is your personal balance between solo time and social collaboration. Some people feel most energized when they're deep in focused, uninterrupted work. Others light up when they're around people, bouncing ideas and building energy through interaction.

To what degree are you energized by each of these?

Maybe you're the kind of person who gets in flow by being on your own. You probably find open-plan offices, constant pings, or too many meetings draining. If that's you, start by carving out what you need:

- In a remote role? Block calendar time that signals "deep focus" and turn off notifications.

- In a hybrid role? Find a quiet corner, use noise-canceling headphones, or book a meeting room, just for solo work.

- In an office? Try arriving early or scheduling desk time away from the busy zones.

> "When I work in a noisy office with constant Slack pings, I lose two hours just trying to refocus. But when I block out 90 minutes of solo time, I fly through my to-dos."
> —Aisha, 24, product designer

If collaboration gives you life, don't let an overly solo setup stall your momentum.

- In a remote setup, schedule virtual co-working blocks or spontaneous "jam" sessions.
- In-office? Seek out teammates who love to problem-solve out loud—or head to a buzzing café where the energy around you can act like creative fuel.

You'll find energy by creating space for shared thinking.

The goal isn't to eliminate the things that occasionally drain you. It's to intentionally build your week around the environment where your energy spikes, and balance the rest with care.

Make it easy for people to communicate with you

Now, let's look at how you prefer to take in information. If you've ever felt like your brain just *doesn't get it* in a meeting, it might not be the content; it might be the format.

Some of us prefer to see it. Slides, visual layouts, whiteboards—anything that lets us map the idea visually. Others need to hear it. We understand best when someone explains it out loud or when we can talk through ideas to clarify them.

Some of us process best by reading: give us a doc or even a well-structured message, and we're good. Others? We don't get it until we've *done* it. We need to be hands-on: testing, prototyping, and trialing to make sense of it all.

There's no wrong way. But the hack is knowing *your* way and helping others know it, too. Whether you ask for the brief in writing, sketch a concept out, or say, "Can we talk this through out loud?"—that one shift can unlock better results with way less effort.

Figure out what you need to start new projects

Everyone has a different entry point into a project. Some of us need to understand the why: the concept, the thesis, or the purpose behind the work. Others need structure: clear steps, timelines, and who's doing what.

And then there are those who just want to jump in and figure it out as they go. Action first. Learn-by-doing.

The question is, what gets *you* into momentum?

If you're concept-driven, block time up front to clarify the purpose. Write it down. Get others aligned. If structure is your preference, use a checklist, a timeline, or a task board to organize your thoughts. And if you need to just start doing something, do that! Build a quick prototype or take the first small step.

Don't let anyone tell you there's one right way to begin. Start where you spark; this is how you will gather your momentum.

Do you work best when you own the project or when you share it?

Some of us love knowing what we own. We want clear accountability. We thrive when we can drive something from start to finish and put our name on it.

Others thrive in shared responsibility. We get energy from collective ownership, being able to jump in, support each other, and co-create.

If you prefer sole responsibility, your productivity hack is clarity. Ask for clear swim lanes and handovers. Use tools that track accountabilities. Ensure you find clarity on your autonomy.

If shared responsibility is your thing, find teams and volunteer to jump into live projects. Collaborate openly and check in often.

When you're set up to work in the style that suits you, you don't just move faster—you move with less friction and with more flow.

How much routine (or variety) do you need to stay energized?

Do you like predictability, or do you get bored fast?

Some people love routine. Familiarity helps them focus. They like knowing what's coming and experiencing consistency over time.

Others need things to evolve—just enough variation to stay engaged, but not so much that it's chaotic.

Then there are those who crave constant newness. Give them a blank canvas, a fresh challenge, or a big unknown to solve—and they're all in.

The hack? Know where you land. And if you're in a role that doesn't match, try rebalancing:

- Add one repeating ritual to stabilize your week
- Propose one small innovation to spark novelty
- Alternate weeks with deep focus and creative chaos

Get your ratio right for you, and you'll avoid both boredom and burnout, but importantly, find your mojo and unlock your creativity.

How do you make decisions (and protect your energy while you do)?

Let's talk about how you make decisions, because this affects your energy way more than you think.

If you're someone who trusts your gut, you'll likely feel confident moving forward once something *feels* right. But if you tend to look for outside input, you may want to see the data, get feedback, or get consensus first.

Neither is better. But knowing your pattern helps. Gut-trusting? Block noise so you can hear your own voice and point of view. External point of view seeker? Build in space to ask questions or check perspectives from data or key stakeholders *before* you decide.

Then, look at the *speed* at which you make decisions. Some people like to move fast. Others want to pause, analyze, and then go. Understand this about yourself and others so that you align your roles and focus areas with your speed to decide.

Finally, what convinces you during decision-making? Some people need to see multiple examples before they can be confident enough to make a decision. Others need a set amount of time: anything from a few minutes to several months, depending on the context. Some can make a call after only partial exposure to something, locking down on a decision right then and there without needing further proof. And then there are those who are never quite convinced—always double-checking, always staying a little skeptical, and checking over your decisions.

Understanding how you make decisions helps you work with your natural energy, not against it. And that's the real productivity hack: fewer moments of internal resistance, more moments of flow.

Don't just delegate tasks, delegate decisions

Let's come back to the big energy leak: those 35,000 decisions a day. They're one of the biggest energy drains. Tiny, constant decisions. What to reply, when to meet, how to prioritize. It's like app-switching for your brain—and it adds up fast.

Research shows the cost is huge. "Ineffective decisions waste more than 500,000 days of managers' time every year in a typical Fortune 500 company."[37] Often, it's not that decisions are especially complex; it's the sheer volume that overwhelms.

Here's where your AI teammate can step in—not just to do things, but to think through the small stuff and streamline your day. It can:

- Filter your messages so you see what matters first.
- Recap your standups and highlight blockers.

- Push key actions to the right tools—no double-handling.
- Auto-batch your calendar based on how you work best.
- Suggest what to focus on (and when) based on your motivation style.
- Summarize meeting notes into themes, decisions, and emotional undercurrents.

Not using productivity hacks yet? Start by building a few defaults:

- No meetings before 10 am
- "Focus blocks" every Wednesday
- Auto-replies that give you thinking time
- Frameworks like the Eisenhower Matrix or OKRs can be used to structure decisions

Even Steve Jobs and Mark Zuckerberg wore the same style of clothes each day to reduce decision fatigue.

And here's where productivity hacks get even more interesting. The future of AI at work isn't just reactive. It's predictive.

Soon, AI won't just summarize decisions—it will help *surface patterns*. Imagine your system nudging you:

- "This topic has come up five times without resolution. Want help deciding?"
- "Energy dipped mid-meeting. Schedule a check-in?"

Your AI teammate will become a context-aware partner in team clarity, helping you align faster, make smarter decisions, and stay more connected.

Well-being rituals: Protect what fuels you

Let's not forget the other half of productivity: *recovery*. High performers don't just sprint—they rest with intention. Well-being rituals are small, consistent habits that give your nervous system what it needs to recharge.

They might look like a two-minute mood check-in, a one-line journal entry to capture a win, or even a midday reset after a tough meeting. These micro-rituals create emotional recovery points so you're not carrying yesterday's stress into tomorrow's priorities.

> "Well-being rituals give your nervous system the break it needs to recover, so you can show up tomorrow without running on fumes."
> —Dan Negroni

Want to take it further? Start with what fuels your body. That might include:

- Protein at every meal to sustain energy
- Eating when your body needs it—some eat every two to three hours, others less often
- Hydration habits like drinking water every hour or hydration drinks
- Avoiding sugar crashes or energy drink slumps that mess with your focus

- Daily meditation or other mindfulness activities like Qi Gong and Yoga

- Weekly fitness from the gym to other activities like running, walking, hiking, etc.

Your AI teammate can support you here too:

- "Why do I feel so tired today?"

- "Help me reframe this frustration."

- "I just got harsh feedback—what's one step I can take forward?"

- "Build me a well-being reset I can do in three minutes."

These rituals might seem small, but they're what make high performance sustainable. Protect what fuels you, and your productivity will follow.

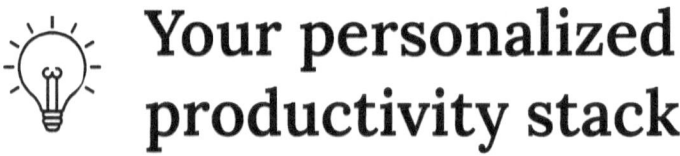 Your personalized productivity stack

You don't need a one-size-fits-all productivity system. You need a work rhythm that matches you. Productivity is about *alignment*. When your daily tasks match your ideal work style, everything flows more easily. When they don't? That's when you stall, procrastinate, or burn out trying to keep up with systems built for someone else.

So let's redesign how you work, starting with your *Productivity* Board.

Step 1: Create your *Productivity* Board

 Head to Marlee.com, click on *Boards*, and create your *Productivity* Board. This will instantly generate a visual summary of the motivational traits that shape how you work best, from your ideal work environment (*Solo* or *Group*) to your preference for how responsibility is shared, how you like to make decisions, and how you prefer to take action.

As you view your visualized productivity charts, reflect on the following:

- What do you notice about your work environment drivers?
- Are you more energized working solo or as part of a structured group?
- Do you feel more engaged when you own a task completely or when you share responsibility with others?

- How often do you need input from others before making decisions?

This is your productivity manual—your personalized guide to how motivation fuels your workflow. These are preferences backed by more than two decades of global research into what drives performance and energy at work.

_____

_____

_____

Step 2: Audit your ways of working

Now bring awareness to how your current work life lines up with what you just saw.

For one week, take note of moments when:

- You feel naturally "in the zone" or focused
- You feel scattered, slowed down, or second-guessing yourself

Then ask yourself:

- *Am I spending too much—or not enough—of my time around groups of people based on my work environment preference?*
- *Do I thrive on autonomy, but find myself bogged down in committee-based decisions?*

- Am I being asked to lead a project solo when I prefer shared ownership (or vice versa)?

_____

_____

_____

_____

These are examples of motivational misalignments. The goal isn't to fix you. It's to align the system around you.

Step 3: Align one habit to your motivation

Now pick *one* pattern from Step 2 that's out of sync, and realign it.

Let's say:

- You prefer solo deep work, but you're constantly pulled into brainstorming sessions. Could you shift some of your creative work into protected solo blocks?

- You prefer shared responsibility, but your projects are managed solo end-to-end. Could you suggest a co-pilot or project buddy to split ownership?

- You thrive with external reference, but you're left to figure things out solo. Could you build in more frequent check-ins or feedback loops?

Start with a small shift—one meeting, one project, one calendar block—and use what you now know about your motivational style to guide the redesign.

___

___

___

___

> "Once I realized I needed structure and shared ownership to stay motivated, I started leading our team's sprints differently. Less chaos, more clarity."
> —Amira, 25, UX designer

Step 4: Set a ritual that reinforces alignment

Create a small weekly ritual that reinforces your productivity preferences. Keep it light, consistent, and aligned to how you naturally work best.

Some ideas:

- **If you prefer group work:** schedule a midweek 15-minute sync to co-work or swap updates.
- **If you prefer solo time:** block a "No Meetings Monday" hour for your most energizing tasks.

- **If you rely on external input:** end the week with a five-minute *Ask Marlee* check-in.

    Try: "What energizes me and what leaves me drained?"

_____

_____

_____

_____

"You're not unproductive, you're just working in ways that don't match your wiring. Let's change that."

—Coach Marlee

Ready to design a more energizing way to work?

The key to sustainable productivity is smarter design. And it starts with you.

By aligning your rituals, tools, and work habits with your natural motivations, you've begun creating a work life where flow isn't rare—it's routine.

But energy alone isn't enough. If you're curious about stepping into greater impact, visibility, or influence, there's one path worth exploring next: leadership.

Up next: We'll show you how to close your leadership gaps—and how your motivation map can help you lead in a way that feels natural, not forced.

CHAPTER 14

Step Up and Lead: Closing the Leadership Gap

TL;DR

The future needs leaders like you.

Leadership roles are opening up, and Gen Z has the chance to step in. But hesitation and old models still hold many back.

- **A global leadership gap is coming:** opportunity is waiting, are you ready to step in?
- **Gen Z leads differently:** purpose, collaboration, and flexibility are your edge.
- **Four leadership blockers to overcome:** Gen Z is less likely to trust their judgment, speak up, take initiative, or think strategically. These are human skills you can develop.
- **Lead in small, powerful ways:** make one confident decision a day.
- **Build your leadership path with Marlee:** use *Ask Marlee* for feedback, start coaching programs, and use *Boards* to compare your traits with a mentor's to learn from the best.

The leadership deficit: Why your future depends on leadership now

By the time you reach the prime of your work life, the world will be facing a global leadership crisis. Leadership roles are opening faster than ever, but the people ready to step into them are in short supply. A serious leadership deficit is emerging, and what happens next depends on whether you and your generation step forward to fill the gap.

The workforce is shifting rapidly. Many Baby Boomers, who've historically held the majority of senior leadership roles, are retiring in large numbers, with more than 11,200 Americans reaching retirement age every day.[38] At the same time, 85 million jobs could go unfilled by 2030 due to a shortage of skilled talent, and leadership roles are among the hardest to replace.[39]

But this isn't just about vacancies, it's about what we lose when leadership disappears. Leadership is what keeps businesses, industries, and societies moving forward. It provides clarity in the chaos, direction through ambiguity, mentoring during stretch moments, and calm in conflict. It's what makes workplaces human. Without it, teams drift, purpose thins out, and even the most talented individuals struggle to grow.

"Organizations without strong leadership at every level will struggle to innovate and stay ahead in a fast-changing world."

—Sundar Pichai, CEO of Google

And yet, just as organizations urgently need fresh leadership, fewer young people are preparing to step into these roles. *The Gen Z at Work Study* found that Gen Z isn't aspiring to traditional leadership positions in the same way as earlier generations did. Instead, Gen Z tends to value collaboration over hierarchy—a powerful shift in mindset, but one that leaves many companies wondering: *Who will drive the future of work?*

This leadership gap is opening new doors, but only for those ready to walk through them. The question isn't whether leadership roles will be available. It's whether you'll be ready to lead in a way that feels energizing, meaningful, and true to who you are.

Why this moment matters: What happens if no one leads?

So what happens if no one steps up to lead?

At first, it doesn't always look like a crisis. It looks like missed signals. Slack threads full of confusion. Team projects that never quite land. People second-guess themselves, not because they don't care, but because no one's painting a clear picture of what's possible.

And over time, that quiet friction turns into something much bigger. Not just a skills gap, or a decision-making gap—but a *human* gap.

Without leaders to champion purpose, workplaces start to feel hollow. Without people willing to speak up for what's right, ethical shortcuts become the norm. Without leaders who actively invite in different perspectives, we risk building futures that leave people out or leave them behind. And when no one is modeling calm, confident leadership in high-pressure moments, anxiety fills the space instead.

This doesn't just impact your job. It shapes how your team shows up, how your family experiences financial security, and how we respond to mental health, climate, and inequality. Whether it's in a group chat, a community, or a global company, *leadership is how humans organize hope.*

And right now, that hope is up for grabs.

What you gain when you lead

Choosing to lead means unlocking more possibilities, especially for you.

When you look at what drives many Gen Zers—purpose, people, sustainability, and flexibility[25]—leadership becomes one of the most powerful ways to bring those values to life. It's about stepping into the kind of influence that feels meaningful and energizing.

Here's what opens up when you decide to lead on your own terms

You gain more impact

You don't just do the work—you shape how it gets done. You help set the tone, influence outcomes, and shift culture from the inside. Whether you're rethinking a process, guiding a team, or pushing for something better, leadership lets you put your fingerprint on the future.

You build a deeper connection

When you lead with empathy, you create space for others to feel safe, supported, and seen. You become someone people trust, not because you have a title, but because you show up with care. That kind of trust creates real belonging, and it changes how teams work together.

You drive ethical, sustainable change

Leadership gives you a seat at the table where priorities are shaped. You can speak up about values, challenge greenwashing, advocate for inclusive policies, and help build systems that serve people, not only profit. The most meaningful change often happens from within, and your voice matters.

You grow faster, inside and out

Stepping into leadership stretches you. You learn how to communicate clearly, stay grounded under pressure, make thoughtful decisions, and trust yourself. These are skills you'll use everywhere—not just in your role, but in life.

You gain more freedom and flexibility

Leaders help design the workday, not just survive it. You can advocate for balance, shape team culture, and create environments that energize instead of deplete. You don't have to wait for a better workplace; you can help build one.

And maybe most important of all, you don't have to become someone else to lead. You just have to start showing up as someone others can trust.

> "The most fulfilling work lives won't be found.
> They'll be built by the people brave enough to lead."
> —Brené Brown, researcher, author, and speaker

But knowing what you gain from leadership doesn't always make the leap feel easier. If you've ever hesitated to speak up, second-guessed your decisions, or waited to be asked, you're not alone. That's what we'll explore next.

The leadership gap: What's stopping you from stepping up?

You're not alone if you've ever thought, *I'm not ready for that yet*. The truth is, most people aren't, but the best leaders act anyway. *The Gen Z at Work Study* found that Gen Z scores significantly lower than earlier generations in four key leadership traits. Let's talk about what these are—and what they look like in real life.

Lack of trust in your personal judgment

One of the biggest barriers to leadership isn't skill; it's hesitation. *The Gen Z at Work Study* found a massive 60% drop in Gen Z's motivation to rely on personal judgment. This means many of you are holding back, waiting for reassurance, and checking in with others before making a call. Sound familiar?

Think of leadership like navigating an escape room. You don't get to sit back and ask someone else for the answer—you make your best call, see what works, and adjust. The more you wait for the "right answer," the longer you stay stuck.

In your work life, Amazon's one-way vs. two-way door decision model is a great framework to apply.

> "Some decisions are one-way doors—big, irreversible moves that require deep thought and careful deliberation. But most decisions aren't like that. They're two-way doors, meaning they're reversible—you can step through, assess the outcome, and course-correct if needed."
> —Jeff Bezos, founder of Amazon

Leaders who understand this difference move faster, innovate more, and avoid getting paralyzed by indecision.

> "As organizations expand, they often start treating all decisions like one-way doors, slowing themselves down unnecessarily."
> —Jeff Bezos, founder of Amazon

The same thing happens in our work lives when we overanalyze every choice. The key to confident leadership is knowing when to take your time and when to just step through the door and adjust as you go. The best leaders don't waste energy on reversible decisions. They act, learn, and refine along the way.

Think about the last time you struggled to make a decision at work. What held you back? Was it fear of being wrong? Worrying about what others would think? Or were you simply overwhelmed by too many options?

> "The workplace is evolving at a speed we've never seen before. The leaders who thrive will be the ones who embrace technology, not fear it, but also the ones who trust themselves enough to make strong, confident decisions without always waiting for a green light from someone else."
> —Dan Negroni

Want to practice? Choose one low-stakes decision each day to make on your own. It could be something as simple as deciding how to structure your workflow or making the call on a project direction. Write it down. Track how it turns out.

Notice when your gut instinct was right and when it wasn't, and reflect on what you learned rather than whether you were "wrong." The more decisions you make, the more trust you'll build in yourself. Confidence grows from doing, not waiting.

To take it further, you don't need to block out hours for a coaching session to strengthen your decision-making. Log in to the Marlee.com app, click *Coaching*, and start your first *Trust Your Gut* program. We'll guide you through small, confidence-building choices on demand. One step at a time, you'll learn how to lead without overthinking.

Reluctance to influence

Leadership isn't about having all the answers. It's about being the one who gets the conversation moving.

The Gen Z at Work Study found that Gen Z has a 40% decline in motivation to influence decisions compared to earlier generations. If you're not putting your ideas forward, someone else is, and sometimes with less insight than you.

Building influence is a lot like growing a social media presence. If you never post, engage, or share your perspective, no one will notice you. This doesn't mean dominating conversations. It means offering your perspective early and clearly.

Try going first in a meeting or suggesting a solution when others stay quiet. If that feels uncomfortable, start by adjusting how you speak. Swap "I think maybe we should . . ." with "Here's what I recommend and why." Small shifts like this change how people perceive your presence and how you see yourself.

Power isn't about control, it's about impact. Leaders who consistently speak up, contribute ideas, and take ownership are more likely to stand out. Research shows that self-confidence and proactive contribution are closely linked to career growth and leadership opportunities. When you believe in your ideas and back them with action, people notice, and they're more likely to see you as someone ready to lead.[40]

> "Great leaders don't just navigate change, they create it. The key is balancing adaptability with strategic clarity."
> —Dan Negroni

Amanda Gorman didn't lead by climbing the corporate ladder—she used her voice, vision, and values to inspire millions. At 22, she stood on the global stage, delivering "The Hill We Climb" at the 2021 US presidential inauguration. With her words, she influenced millions, not by commanding, but by connecting.

> "You don't have to be a poet, you don't have to be a politician, or be in the White House to make an impact with your words. We all have this capacity to find solutions for the future."
> —Amanda Gorman, poet and activist

Her story reminds us that leadership is often about sharing a vision others can feel and follow. You don't need permission to influence. You need intention and the courage to speak.

Hesitation to take initiative

Compared to earlier generations, Gen Z is 44% less motivated to act without permission. That shows up as waiting for someone to assign you a task, hesitating to raise your hand, or not stepping up when there's a gap to fill. But the leaders who rise fast? They start things. They don't wait for an invite. Leadership requires action, not just analysis. If you always wait for the perfect moment, you'll miss the best opportunities.

Think of Ava. She's a 26-year-old founder who started a remote-first company without ever managing a traditional team. She built her business across five countries using digital tools and a collaborative culture, not a corporate playbook.

> "I never saw leadership as being about authority. For me, it's about empowering others and ensuring diverse perspectives lead to better solutions."
> —Ava, 26, program manager

Great leaders are self-starters. Mark Zuckerberg didn't wait for permission to disrupt an industry—he built Facebook from his college dorm room, testing early versions and launching fast before he had a full business plan. He didn't have all the answers, but he had the initiative to start.

Malala Yousafzai, at 11, began advocating for girls' education in Pakistan—not because someone gave her permission, but because she saw a need and acted.

> "One child, one teacher, one book, and one pen can change the world."
> **—Malala Yousafzai, activist and Nobel laureate**

When you take initiative, you're not just moving things forward; you're signaling that you're ready to lead. That's when people start to notice. Think about the last time you saw an opportunity to step up but held back. What stopped you? Was it the fear of getting it wrong? Feeling like someone else was "more qualified"?

Here's your challenge: Next time you see something that needs doing, step in before you're asked. Offer to lead a discussion, take charge of a project, or put forward an idea without waiting for an invitation. You'll be surprised how quickly people start seeing you as a leader, not because you have all the answers, but because you're willing to initiate something new when others hesitate.

Lack of big-picture thinking

Execution gets you noticed. Strategic thinking gets you trusted. But *The Gen Z at Work Study* found a 53% decline in motivation for big-picture thinking in Gen Z compared to earlier generations. That means many of you are excellent at completing tasks but not yet connecting them to the bigger vision.

Big-picture thinking is about seeing how your work fits into the wider ecosystem. It's about asking, "What's the bigger shift we're driving here?" or "How does this decision impact what happens next quarter—or next year?"

Boyan Slat didn't just create a product—he imagined a future where oceans were free of plastic. That clarity gave his work meaning and direction.

> "You don't have to be an expert to make a difference, you just have to care."
> —Boyan Slat, inventor and founder of The Ocean Cleanup

Or think of Steve Jobs. At the core of his vision was the belief that technology should not only be functional but also seamlessly integrated into daily life. That's what big-picture thinking does. It connects purpose to execution.

To develop this skill, pause at the start of each week and ask *What's the strategic purpose behind my top three priorities? Where is this heading? Who does this impact?* Strategic thinking starts with reflection, not with having all the answers.

 Shape your personal leadership path

You don't have to wait for someone to tell you you're a leader. If you've started speaking up, making decisions, or lifting others, you've already begun. Now it's about building self-awareness, refining your style, and growing into the kind of leader you want to become.

Let's walk through a few powerful ways you can start shaping your leadership path, on your terms.

Step 1: *Ask Marlee* the big questions

 Discover your leadership potential and where you sometimes hold back, so you can lead with confidence instead of comparison.

Log in to the Marlee.com app, then head to *Ask Marlee* and type:

- "What are my strengths and blind spots as a leader?"
- "What can make me a better leader?"

_____

_____

_____

Step 2: Start a leadership coaching program (or two)

Take the journey to develop yourself as a leader. Marlee's AI coaching programs are built around you and your goals, designed to fit into your schedule with short, practical sessions that meet you where you are today.

 Visit Marlee.com, click *Coaching*, and choose one of Marlee's free AI-powered leadership programs to begin building skills in real time:

- **Personal Power:** communicate with confidence, influence with clarity.

- **Goal Catcher:** learn how to motivate yourself and others around a shared mission.

- **Start Fast:** take initiative and act without waiting for permission.

- **Big Picture Thinker:** connect your daily tasks to long-term goals and impact.

Take notes as you go through your first leadership coaching program

_____

_____

_____

_____

Step 3: Learn from a leader you admire

Have a mentor, teammate, or manager whose leadership you respect? Invite them to Marlee. Once connected, go to *Boards* and create a 1 to 1 Board to compare your traits side by side.

Then *Ask Marlee*:

- "What are @Ronan and my similarities and differences?"

You'll get a breakdown of where you align and which of their standout traits you might want to grow toward. This is your chance to study and model great leadership up close, then build your own version of it.

Remember, leadership is a path you design as you go based on your values, your energy, and the impact you want to have.

You don't have to map it all out right now. You just have to take the next step.

Drop notes on what you learn from their style

_____

_____

_____

_____

_____

Your leadership evolution starts now

Leadership isn't something that happens to you. It's something you decide to do, be, and grow into, through action, self-awareness, and intention. If you've made it this far or started one of Marlee's leadership coaching programs, you're already on the path.

You've begun developing the traits that matter most: trusting your judgment, speaking up, taking initiative, and thinking strategically. These are the foundations of modern leadership—and they grow stronger with each step you take.

As you move forward, remember: leadership is about choosing what to lead, and how to lead it, in a way that feels energizing, not exhausting.

Up next: You'll start using your *Marlee Workverse Map*—a simple but powerful tool to turn *everything* you've learned into action. It helps you design a work life that fuels your energy, plays to your strengths, and supports the kind of leader you want to become.

You're not just stepping up. You're stepping into alignment.

CHAPTER 15

Build Your Life with Real Meaning

TL;DR

Clarity is your compass.

When you design your life around what energizes you, meaning and fulfillment follow. This chapter turns your insights into action, using the *Marlee Workverse Map* as your guide.

- **Find your through line:** a deeper mission that anchors choices and brings focus when things feel overwhelming.
- **Track your energy:** spot what fuels you and what drains you.
- **Align your actions:** connect daily steps to your deeper why.
- **Catch burnout early:** notice the signs and course-correct with confidence.
- **Design your rhythm:** create visibility, flexibility, and flow across your work life.

You've got the insight, now it's time to build your life

You've uncovered what drives you. You've explored how to lead, grow, and work in flow. Now comes the part that ties it all together. This chapter is your integration point—a space to map your Workverse in a way that's energizing, personal, and practical. Not someone else's version of success. Yours. This is about showing up with clarity, alignment, and self-leadership. One decision at a time.

> "Self-leadership is your anchor in a shifting world. Your *Marlee Workverse Map* helps you design a life that energizes you."
> —**Michelle Duval**

Before you dive in and start building your *Marlee Workverse Map*, take a moment to choose your way: you can write directly onto these pages, or scan the QR code to create your own virtual version via the Marlee Workverse Map template in Canva.

It's a flexible, living artifact—something you'll return to, update, and evolve over time. Whether you're seeking clarity, energy, or a path that feels more like you, this map is your tool for designing a life with meaning, not just momentum.

What is the *Marlee Workverse Map*?

 Create your Workverse Map! It's your compass to stay energized and make choices that feel right.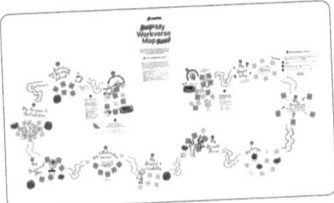

 Scan the QR code or visit Marlee.com/workverse

Think of this as the moment you step into your own arena. The place where your rhythm gets clear, your direction sharpens, and your next move starts to mean something.

In every iconic story, there's a moment when everything shifts. Not because the hero is ready, but because they care too deeply not to act. That moment reveals their *through line*. The inner force that drives their choices, shapes their path, and pulls them forward when everything else feels uncertain.

When Miles Morales is pulled into the multiverse in *Spider-Verse*, he doesn't know how to be Spider-Man. He just knows he has to try. His through line? To believe he belongs in the story, before the world does. Each leap is a bet on his future self.

When Katniss Everdeen volunteers in *The Hunger Games*, she doesn't rise because she wants to. She rises because someone she loves is in danger. Her through line? Protect, no matter the cost. That quiet instinct becomes a full-blown uprising. A girl who won't stay silent.

When Harry Potter steps into Hogwarts, he's not dreaming of greatness. He just wants a place to belong. His through line? Connection. Loyalty. Courage over comfort. Every choice he makes flows from that longing to protect what feels like home.

That's what your through line is. It's not a goal. It's the heartbeat beneath your decisions. A rhythm you follow, even when the path ahead feels blurry.

The *Marlee Workverse Map* helps you find *your* rhythm—and follow it.

It's your quest compass.

It's how you move with clarity in a Workverse that won't stop shifting.

And it's how you shape a life that feels right for *you*, choice by choice, step by step.

Why create your map?

A map is about creating signposts—to help you stay on *your* track, not someone else's.

Katniss didn't follow the Capitol's rules. She rewrote them. Harry didn't walk a pre-approved path—he chose loyalty over legacy. And Miles didn't wait for a mentor to hand him a plan. He created his own swing.

Your Marlee Workverse Map is how you do the same. It helps you lead with alignment, not autopilot.

Creating your map helps you:

- Spot what energizes you—and what drains you
- Align your daily actions with your deeper quest
- Catch burnout before it hits
- Say yes to what moves you forward—and no to what pulls you off track

- Track your own evolution, so your work life grows with you

This is about clarity. Your map doesn't tell you where to go. It helps you move forward with purpose, rhythm, and flow.

> "This is your time to lead with clarity. Your growth becomes real the moment you decide to own it."
> —Dan Negroni

How to use your map

Great maps not only show you *where* to go, they help you remember *why you're going*.

Use this map like Katniss used her instincts, like Harry trusted his circle, like Miles followed his swing—even when the path wasn't clear yet.

This isn't a vision board you make once and forget. It's a living framework to help you design your week, shape your habits, filter your decisions, and stay connected to what lights you up.

Here's how to use it:

- **Each morning:** check your map before diving into tasks. Are you choosing from alignment or reacting to noise?
- **Each week:** reset your focus. What gave you energy? What needs to shift?
- **Each month:** update a section. Has your motivation changed? Have your values evolved?

- **When making decisions:** ask *Does this move me closer to who I'm becoming?*
- **When stuck:** reconnect to your through line. Let it guide your next move.

Your map grows as you do. Let it guide you, not define you. Let it hold your rhythm. And when things get noisy, let this be the signal that brings you back to yourself.

Let's go

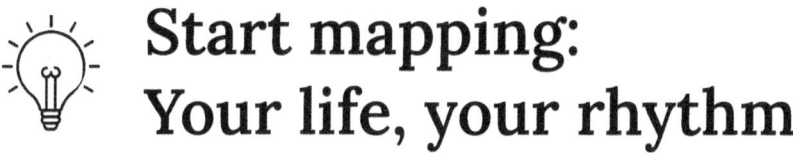 Start mapping: Your life, your rhythm

These 11 steps help you reflect, realign, and move forward with confidence. Use it daily, weekly, or whenever you feel pulled off track. You don't need to know exactly where you're going—just that you're building in a direction that feels right for you.

Step 1: My motivational drivers

What naturally energizes me at work and in life?

This step helps you uncover what truly energizes you so you can stop working against yourself and start moving in flow.

What are my top five motivations? Where do they show up in my work or life?

_____

_____

_____

What energizes me, based on my Marlee results?

Which other motivational *Bubbles* light me up in the app?

_____

_____

_____

What patterns do I see across work, study, or side projects?

_____

_____

_____

_____

. . . .

Bring it to life → Take action now:
Spot the motivations that fuel your flow.

- Head to Marlee.com → log in → My Profile & Results → All Motivations → Bubbles.

- Star your top five, note where they already show up (work/study/side projects).

. . . .

Step 2: My deeper why

What threads run through the moments that matter most to me?

This step helps you uncover the deeper values, causes, and inner drives that shape your decisions and define how you want to contribute to the world. It's about noticing the patterns that keep showing up in your stories, your actions, and your instincts.

What stories do I find myself telling again and again—what do they reveal?

_____

_____

_____

_____

_____

What's a problem or puzzle I'd be willing to work on for the rest of my life?

_____

_____

_____

_____

_____

What have I stood up for (or walked away from) because it truly mattered?

_____

_____

_____

_____

_____

If I looked at the most meaningful moments of my life so far, what connects them?

_____

_____

_____

_____

_____

Bring it to life → Take action now:
Turn meaningful moments into a map of what you value.

- Experiment with reflective journaling: use *Voice* notes in Notion or the *Notes* app to track stories, reactions, or moments that feel meaningful.

- Then head to Marlee.com → *Ask Marlee* and type: "What motivates me?" You'll get a clear snapshot of the drivers behind your choices.

- Finally, go to *Boards* → Create your *Future Roles Board*. Click *Generate Insights*. This connects the dots between what you care about and the environments that bring those values to life. You'll see how your motivations align with the "ideal zone," and discover roles and industries where your values and energy naturally fuel your impact.

Step 3: My direction

Where am I heading, and what matters most?

This step helps you connect with what you're really building toward—not just goals, but your deeper direction.

What's the work or life direction I feel pulled toward?

_____

_____

_____

What values guide my decisions, even when things get hard?

_____

_____

_____

_____

What keeps showing up again and again—an idea, a cause, a need?

_____

_____

_____

_____

• •

Bring it to life → Take action now:
Translate what matters most into a clear path forward.

- Head to Marlee.com → *Ask Marlee* and type: "What industries suit my motivations?" or "What roles suit my motivations?"

- You'll get tailored insights that link your motivational strengths to real-world paths.

• •

Step 4: My energy patterns

What rhythms, roles, and environments help me thrive?

When your energy is in sync with your tasks and space, work gets lighter and more productive.

Do I work best alone, in pairs, or in a group?

_____

_____

_____

What kind of flow works for me—sprints, long blocks, or flexibility?

_____

_____

_____

What routines help me stay steady without burning out?

_____

_____

_____

_____

_____

Bring it to life → Take action now:
Spot the patterns behind your best energy.

- Head to Marlee.com → *Boards* → Create your *Work Environment* Board and explore how your motivations shape the spaces and rhythms that help you thrive.

- Keep a *Work Style Tracker*—even a quick daily journal or voice note—on when you felt most "in the zone" and when you didn't.

- Pair this with simple *Energy Reboot Rituals* (like a five-minute walk, playlist, or reset stretch) to recover faster and keep your flow steady.

Step 5: My growth focus

Where am I growing, and how can I flex without losing flow?

Growth feels best when it's aligned. This step keeps your development personal and powerful.

What am I learning or improving right now?

_____
_____
_____
_____

What skill or trait do I want to be known for in the next year?

___

___

___

___

Where am I hiding in comfort—and how could I gently step out?

___

___

___

___

....

Bring it to life → Take action now:
Identify your growth edge with clarity.

- Head to Marlee.com → *Boards* → Create your *Human Skills (Soft Skills)* Board and see what's sitting in your ideal zone and what's outside it. That gap is your growth edge.

- Need support building it? Jump into *Coaching* → Start *Multiply Your Impact*. Short, practical sessions help you flex new skills without burning out.

- Want to explore beyond work? Try something new that stretches you, like Mindvalley Quests on peak performance or well-being. Think of it as experimenting outside your comfort zone while still staying aligned with what energizes you.

....

Step 6: My visibility and impact

How do I show up, and how is my work seen by others?

Visibility isn't about being loud—it's about being clear, intentional, and connected to your impact. Visibility helps others see your potential—and helps you own it.

Where have I influenced a group, project, or person this month?

_____

_____

_____

_____

What's my natural way of leading—collaborative, directive, behind the scenes?

_____

_____

_____

_____

Where do I want to be more visible or recognized?

_____

_____

_____

_____

Bring it to life → Take action now:
See a clear picture of how you lead, and where you can grow.

Head to Marlee.com → *Boards* → Open your *Human Skills (Soft Skills)* Board and explore charts like *Holding others accountable, Asserting boundaries and needs,* and *Compelling culture.* These give you a mirror of how others experience you, and where small shifts could amplify your impact.

Then, choose one way to step forward this week:

- **Networking:** Reach out to someone you admire and start a conversation.

- **Thought leadership:** Share a short reflection or idea on LinkedIn or Threads: let people see what drives you.

- **Public speaking:** Say yes to presenting in class, leading a stand-up, or speaking at an event—practice being visible in the spaces that matter to you.

Step 7: My collaboration patterns

How do I build bridges across work styles and generations?

Collaboration works best when you adapt to others, without losing yourself. The more you understand how different generations communicate, resolve conflict, and lead, the easier it is to build a real connection (and avoid crossed wires).

Where do I experience friction with teammates or leaders?

_____

_____

_____

_____

What communication style works best for me, and how flexible am I?

_____

_____

_____

_____

How can I grow stronger at navigating different expectations or preferences?

_____

_____

_____

_____

••

Bring it to life → Take action now:
Discover the power to understand and bring out the best in teammates from any generation.

- Head to Marlee.com → *Boards* → Create a *Gen X and Me* Board (and do the same for other generations you work with).

- You'll get a side-by-side view of your motivators and theirs, especially around communication styles. It's like having a translation guide for collaboration. You'll know when your approach builds instant trust and where small adjustments can prevent friction.

••

Step 8: My financial flow

How do I earn, save, and build safety on my terms?

When you understand your income rhythm, money stress takes a back seat, and creative freedom expands.

What does financial confidence mean for me right now?

_____

_____

What income sources or rituals help me feel secure? Am I relying too much on one income stream?

_____

_____

Where can I build safety nets for breaks, growth, or unexpected changes?

_____

_____

_____

_____

Bring it to life → Take action now:
Build financial security that frees up your focus.

- Start by creating an *Income Ecosystem Map* → Use a free template in Miro, Canva, or even a notebook sketch to visualize all your income streams. Seeing them side by side helps you spot gaps and opportunities.

- Try YNAB (You Need A Budget) → Give every dollar a job and take the guesswork out of saving.

- Set up a *Freelance/Side Hustle Tracker* → Try Google Sheets, Notion, or a template you love. Tracking gigs, income, and time in one place builds the safety net that lets you create with confidence.

Step 9: My purpose, contribution, and impact

What causes, values, or communities do I care about, and how does my work align?

Purpose keeps your work meaningful, even on hard days. When your day-to-day actions feel connected to something bigger, you're more likely to stay motivated.

_____
_____
_____

Where does my work already contribute to something bigger?

_____
_____
_____

What impact do I want to make—locally, globally, or quietly?

_____
_____
_____

How does this connect to the life I want to lead?

_____

_____

_____

Bring it to life → Take action now:
See how your work adds up to real impact.

- Create an *Impact Alignment Checklist* → List your current projects and reflect on how each one links (or doesn't link) to the causes, values, and communities that matter most to you.

- Explore *AI-for-Good Pathways* → Find projects, tools, or industries where AI is being used to tackle challenges like climate action, equity, or mental well-being. It's a simple way to see how your skills could amplify real-world impact.

Step 10: My boundaries and recovery rituals

How do I protect my energy while staying ambitious?

Work without boundaries leads to burnout. Building a map for rest, rituals, and emotional health gives you longevity, not just short-term wins.

What drains me the fastest, and what helps me recover?

_____

_____

_____

_____

Where do I need to set or strengthen a boundary (with tech, people, work)?

_____

_____

_____

What rituals help me reset weekly, monthly, or mid-project?

_____

_____

_____

Bring it to life → Take action now:
Design rituals that protect your energy and spot burnout before it hits.

- Log in to Marlee.com → *My Profile & Results* → *All Motivations* → *Bubbles*. Notice which motivations fuel you most, then build boundaries that protect them.

- Track your ups and downs with an *Emotional Energy Calendar*, so you can plan around your natural highs and lows.

- Set simple reset cues (like do-not-disturb modes or alarms) and use a *Burnout Flags Checklist* to catch stress early.

Step 11: My next chapter

What shift is emerging, and how do I make space for it?

You're not meant to stay static. This step honors your evolution. Learn how to pause, reflect, and choose your next step.

What feels like it's coming to a close or starting to feel stale?

_____

_____

_____

_____

What part of me wants to emerge next?

_____
_____
_____

What new direction or small experiment could I try?

_____
_____
_____
_____

Bring it to life → Take action now:
Identify and celebrate your growth. Get crystal clear on the next area to focus on.

- Head to Marlee.com → Boards → Create your *Over Time Board* and retake your *Motivational Analysis*. Spot what's shifted: those changes are clues to what's ending and what wants to begin.

- Before you start a new course, job, or project → Revisit your *Marlee Workverse Map*. Sanity-check: mission fit, values fit, energy fit. If it's a "yes," set a 30-day experiment to test it in the real world.

A map that moves with you

The Workverse will keep shifting. But now that you have a map that reflects your energy, values, and evolving direction, you won't get lost, so long as you focus the way you now know how to. You have the space to design from alignment, not pressure. Whether you revisit this once a week or once a season, use your map; it's here to help you stay grounded and keep growing.

Next up: You're not on this journey alone. We hand the map to your mentors, managers, and champions—the *Gen Z Evangelists*. It's their 90-day game plan to support you as you lead from exactly where you are.

Your next step is about doing what matters—with energy, clarity, and confidence.

CHAPTER 16

Empower Gen Z to Thrive: A Guide for Evangelists

TL;DR

Gen Z doesn't need more direction; they need *your* support to lead on their own terms.

This chapter is for the mentors, managers, parents, and coaches who want to empower Gen Z without micromanaging. Gen Z will thrive when you provide:

- **Safety:** to explore, fail, and grow.
- **Balance:** structure without taking away autonomy.
- **Clarity:** communication that guides, not controls.
- **Confidence:** support to build human skills like strategic thinking and influence.
- **Personalized tools:** *Marlee Boards*, *Ask Marlee*, and AI coaching programs that personalize feedback, deepen their self-awareness, and track growth over time.

The future needs champions

You're here because you care. You've seen the potential in Gen Z and you want to be the person who helps them thrive, not just survive, at work. This chapter gives you the tools to do just that, without micromanaging, overexplaining, or guessing.

Gen Z is the most inclusive, purpose-driven, and tech-savvy generation. They're not just shaping the future of work; they're redefining it. But even the most ambitious change makers need support structures that help them turn potential into impact.

That's where you come in.

Whether you're a coach, manager, educator, parent, or mentor, you're a *Gen Z evangelist*. Someone who doesn't just see potential but helps unlock it. Someone who understands that this generation doesn't need more rules; they need frameworks, feedback, and freedom to thrive.

> "This generation doesn't want to be told who to become. They want to be supported in discovering who they already are."
> —Michelle Duval

Gen Z is entering a Workverse unlike anything earlier generations faced. And while their potential is extraordinary, from innovation to social change, many lack the support systems they need to thrive. *The Gen Z at Work Study* found that this generation is highly motivated, but also more likely to pause, seek external input, and second-guess themselves in unfamiliar situations. That means they need clear guidance, encouragement, and regular feedback to build confidence, strengthen human skills, and grow into new challenges.

And here's where the stakes get even higher. If we don't provide that support, we risk a generational leadership vacuum. With Baby Boomers retiring in record numbers, the pipeline of future-ready leaders is thinning fast. Without coaching and mentorship, we could lose a generation of changemakers before they even begin. For Gen Z to rise, they'll need more than encouragement; they'll need people like you in their corner.

So, what does intentional support look like in practice?

> "You don't have to be perfect,
> but you do have to be 100% committed."
> —Alexandria Ocasio-Cortez,
> US Congresswoman

Let's give you a framework to follow, one that helps Gen Z thrive, while keeping your role clear, empowering, and future-focused.

Before we begin, if you've been handed this chapter or are starting the book here, welcome. This chapter was designed to stand alone as a practical guide for Gen Z evangelists, leaders, mentors, parents, and advocates.

If you'd like practical ways to put this chapter into action with a Gen Z in your life, head to Marlee.com to explore the free AI collaboration tools we'll reference throughout. You can create an *Individual Results Board* to see your Gen Zer's unique strengths at a glance, or a *1 to 1 Board* to compare your motivators side by side. These simple, visual tools help you notice where your styles align and where they differ, so your support lands with the biggest impact.

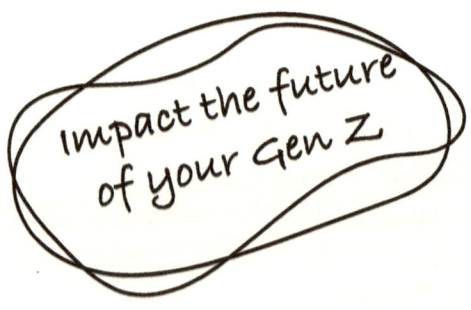

Your 90-day support plan: Help Gen Z thrive

This framework is for you—the manager, mentor, parent, coach, or facilitator who wants to support Gen Z without micromanaging. It's not about stepping in. It's about stepping up in the right moments, asking better questions, and guiding growth in a way that builds trust, motivation, and momentum. Tools like Marlee are here to make that easier, giving you clear insights and language so your support connects in a way that feels personal.

Understanding your role as a Gen Z evangelist

From advice-giver to growth guide

Traditional support often sounds like advice, instructions, or top-down direction. But what Gen Z needs is a partner in their development, a guide who's willing to listen, explore, and co-create growth.

Instead of: "Have you done this yet?"

Try: "What's getting in the way of progress right now?"

Instead of: "Let me tell you how I'd do it . . ."

Try: "Want to walk through options together?"

These shifts build trust, not dependence. And trust is the real accelerator.

Creating psychological safety

Gen Z tends to thrive in environments where they feel safe to take risks, share ideas, and fail forward. Psychological safety is not about shielding them from challenges but about ensuring they have the confidence to engage, ask questions, and innovate without fear of judgment.

How to create psychological safety:

- **Encourage open dialogue:** make sure Gen Z voices are heard and valued. As a generation, they broadly prefer regular feedback. Create space for questions, ideas, and input without immediate judgment or dismissal.

- **Normalize failure as part of learning:** Gen Z is highly motivated by external sources of inspiration and feedback, so share plenty of examples of growth through setbacks, and frame failures as stepping stones to improvement.

- **Model vulnerability:** leaders and mentors who acknowledge their own challenges help create an environment where Gen Z feels comfortable being authentic.

Balancing procedures with autonomy

Gen Z values procedures but rejects micromanagement. They want to understand the procedure to get started and then be given the freedom to execute in ways that work best for them.

As an evangelist, whether you are a mentor, parent, teacher, or coach, you play a critical role in guiding Gen Z to develop sustainable confidence. This requires introducing a procedure via YouTube, a step-by-step recipe or process, and helping them to build confidence in using it.

Navigating when to step in to support with procedures and when to step back to give autonomy is key to building and nurturing confidence. By playing these roles at different stages, you provide both the process they need to feel secure and the autonomy they crave to take ownership of their growth. The goal is to cultivate confidence, resilience, and continuous learning, essential qualities for Gen Z to thrive.

Gen Z communication preferences

Effective communication with Gen Z requires adapting to its digital-first, asynchronous, and feedback-driven style.

Best practices for connecting with Gen Zers:

- **Use asynchronous communication channels:** they prefer reading and writing using messaging platforms (SMS, Slack, WhatsApp, or Discord) over lengthy face-to-face meetings.

- **Provide real-time feedback:** rather than annual or quarterly performance reviews, use continuous feedback loops to encourage growth and ensure they receive weekly support.

- **Keep written messages clear and concise:** vague explanations are often lost. Get to the point, be concrete and specific, and invite questions and discussion.

- **Leverage short-form content for learning:** interactive, bite-sized content, via microlearning platforms or short knowledge-sharing sessions, resonates more than traditional long-form approaches.

Write what you're noticing in their style

_____

_____

_____

Development frameworks that work for Gen Z

Productivity

Focus on outcome-driven work rather than rigid schedules. Gen Z prioritizes efficiency, digital tools, and work-life balance.

Key productivity approaches that work for Gen Z:

- **Task batching and time-blocking:** help them manage deep work without unnecessary context-switching.

- **Flexible workflows:** many prefer working asynchronously when creativity strikes rather than adhering to fixed office hours.

- **Leveraging AI and automation:** Gen Z is quick to adopt tools that eliminate manual tasks and streamline workflows.

- **Well-being rituals as high-performance drivers:** mindfulness, movement, and flexibility aren't "extras" for Gen Z; they're what sustain focus and prevent burnout.

Want to bring it to life? With Marlee's *Productivity* Board, you and your Gen Zer can quickly spot which habits fuel their focus and which ones drain it. That clarity makes it easier to design systems that match their natural energy, not fight against it.

Note what supports their productivity and energy

_____

_____

_____

Growth areas for maximum impact

To maximize their impact at work, Gen Z needs targeted development in areas that will future proof their careers and work lives:

- **Strategic thinking and problem-solving:** help them move beyond immediate, detail-focused tasks to understand broader macro-level business challenges.

- **Resilience and adaptability:** as they enter a workforce shaped by automation, economic shifts, and AI, developing adaptability is crucial.

- **Relationship building:** strengthen interpersonal and collaboration skills, particularly in remote and hybrid work settings.

- **Personal branding and thought leadership:** encourage them to build a digital presence, whether through LinkedIn, content creation, or industry networks.

Note which areas could unlock their next level

_____

_____

_____

Days 1–30: Build trust and understand their motivation

Before any growth happens, Gen Z needs to feel seen and safe. Your first goal is to create that space.

Try this:

- **Ask, don't assume:** use open-ended questions such as "What gives you energy at work?" or "What makes you hesitate?"

- **Use the Marlee *Gen Z and Me* Board:** once you've both completed the *Motivational Analysis*, you'll get a clear picture of how your Gen Zer's motivations compare to their generation. It's a shortcut to spotting what energizes them most, and where they may need extra encouragement.

- **Create a 1 to 1 Board:** this side-by-side view of your motivators and theirs helps you see how your work styles align or differ. It takes the guesswork out of building trust.

- **Ask Marlee:** try prompts such as "How can I provide constructive feedback to @Jamie effectively?" or "What motivates @Jamie?" You'll get instant, tailored guidance that helps your feedback land in a way that feels supportive, without having to rely on trial and error.

- **Ensure feedback feels personal:** reference their motivators and blind spots, not just generic performance comments.

- **Create a feedback loop:** schedule a one-to-one check-in every two weeks. Ask "What's one thing you're proud of this week?" or "What's one thing you'd like to feel more confident in?"

List what you've learned about their motivations

_____

_____

_____

_____

"You don't need to give Gen Z a map. You just need to be the guide who helps them explore what's already possible." **—Dan Negroni**

Days 31-60: Build skills and confidence

Once you've built trust, it's time to challenge them, gently. Help them connect their goals to real momentum.

Try this:

- **Give feedback on what's working well:** communicate what they should keep doing, and how their actions are helping them move toward their goals.

- **Invite them to create their *Human Skills (Soft Skills)* Board in the Marlee app:** it gives you both a clear view of which skills sit in their "ideal zone" and which ones may need strengthening. You might see things such as *Asserting boundaries and needs* or *Decision-making*. Those skills outside the zone aren't weaknesses; they're growth edges where the biggest breakthroughs happen. Click *Generate Insight* together to see personalized guidance behind that skill, so you're not just guessing what to work on, you're starting with insights tailored to how they're wired.

- **Help them choose an achievable goal:** direct them toward these growth areas for the next 30 days. Something like: "Run a team meeting," "Present my own idea," or "Mentor someone new."

- **Point them to one of Marlee's free AI coaching programs that match their growth goal:** each program is like having a bite-sized coach in their pocket, short, practical sessions they can apply immediately at work.

    - Working on influence? Suggest *Personal Power*.

    - Need strategic thinking? Try *Big Picture Thinker*.

- Want to help them start faster? Use *Start Fast*.

- **Encourage weekly progress check-ins:** focus not just on what they did, but on what they learned.

- **When they complete a coaching program,** encourage them to retake their *Motivational Analysis* (or annually). Then, create or update their *Over Time* Board in the Marlee app. This lets them see how their motivations evolve over time, so growth isn't just something they feel, it's something they can track, measure, and celebrate.

Keep the rhythm going:

- **Model tools:** time-blocking, async communication, and energy rituals from Chapter 14.

- **Co-create their work rhythms:** using tools like Sunsama, Notion, or the Marlee app.

Jot down the tactics and takeaways so far

_____

_____

_____

_____

"You're not here to direct every step. You're here to notice what's working and help them develop it."
—Coach Marlee

Days 60-90: Reinforce growth and autonomy

Here's where you step back to reinforce their growth, but not step out. By now, they've seen their own progress. Your job is to create space for them to lead.

Do this:

- **Reflect on what's changed:** ask "What feels easier now? What still feels uncomfortable?"

- **Let them lead your next check-in:** invite them to set the agenda and share what support they still want.

Support autonomy:

- **Encourage them to use Ask *Marlee* to explore fresh questions, such as:** "What are my areas of improvement?" or "How can I improve my blind spots?" The responses give them instant, personalized insights they can return to anytime, so they build self-reliance without losing momentum.

- **Give them visibility:** help them share their wins in team meetings, async channels, or digital boards.

Note how you're stepping back (but staying close)

_____

_____

_____

> "Support doesn't mean stepping in. Sometimes, it means stepping back, just enough for them to find their own rhythm."
> —Coach Marlee

Looking ahead: A shared future

The workplace of 2035 won't run on hierarchy; it will thrive on trust, adaptability, and collaboration between humans and AI. Gen Z is already paving the way, but they can't do it alone.

Support Gen Z with the tools contained here, along with the right mindset and space to grow, and you won't just shape one person's path; you'll help shape the future of work.

We'll See You in the Workverse

You've just done what creators, athletes, innovators, and artists do at their best. You paused long enough to map your motivations, reflect on who you want to become, and imagine a future only you can build. That takes courage. And that's where real change begins.

Now that you've read Workverse, remember: it's most powerful when you make it hyper-personal to you. **This book + Marlee + the tools we've created = your Workverse OS.** Here's how to bring it to life:

1. **See it in action.** Head to marlee.com/workverse and watch our *How to Marlee* video. In 90 seconds, you'll see how to take this playbook and personalize it with Marlee's technology.

2. **Join a live session.** Jump into our monthly *How to Marlee* sessions! These relaxed, open sessions are run by our Community Happiness team, where you can explore the insights behind your results, ask any questions (big or small), and share challenges you're working through at work or in life.

3. **Map your path.** Use our Canva *Workverse Map* template. It's your visual template to revisit anytime—daily, weekly, or whenever you're making a big choice (side gig, new role, work pivot).

4. **Find your people.** Join the Workverse community @MyWorkverse and share your story with #MyWorkverse. We've curated Gen Z stories to inspire you, and we'd love to hear yours, so we can keep supporting you. Tell us what you need or just say hey!

5. **Pass it on.** Share what you've learned; mentor a peer, lead with empathy, or spark a conversation with your team lead, mentor, or even your parents about how to better support Gen Z. This is how your Workverse shifts from me to we.

> "Which of these feels like the right first step for you? Start there. You don't need to do it all at once, just begin."
> **—Coach Marlee**

And remember, you're not alone in this. You've now got your *Individual Results* Board, your AI teammate Marlee, and your unique motivational fingerprint. And you've got us, the humans within Marlee—cheering you on!

> "My vision is a world where every person, no matter who they are, has access to realize their potential. You're already leading that future. Thank you for inviting us on your journey."
> **—Michelle Duval**

"You've got more power than you think. If this book lit even one spark of confidence in you, I hope you run with it. And if I can support you further, find me on LinkedIn. I'm always here for Gen Z."
—**Dan Negroni**

"Let's stay connected. I'll be here whenever you have a question, a reflection, or a next step. Your energy, your values, your Workverse: I'll help you stay aligned with your unique path and goals."
—**Coach Marlee**

Acknowledgments

To Gen Z: our readers, our children, our students, and the teammates we've had the privilege to coach: thank you. You are the heartbeat of this book. We're endlessly inspired by your vision for what work could be and deeply moved by what you've shared with us about what it's like now. You've made us better coaches, better listeners, and more hopeful humans. This book is for you, because of you.

To our friends and families: thank you for making space for the late nights, for tolerating the Post-it notes and the tangents, and for cheering us on even when we weren't always fun to live with. We're especially grateful for the younger ones in our lives, whose potential lit the fire under this whole project. And to our close friends who asked the right questions or simply reminded us to eat, thank you. Your care was the quiet support beneath every page.

To our Workverse collaborators, Jon Whitby and Emily Willis: thank you for your vision, your craft, and your commitment to shaping this book with us. Emily, as our Developmental Editor, you carried Workverse like a personal mission—burning the midnight oil, meticulously refining every idea, and guiding the book's evolution with unwavering care. Your fingerprints are woven through every chapter, from structure to story, and your leadership has been instrumental in bringing Workverse to life.

To our incredible team at Marlee: thank you for turning an ambitious vision into a living technology that brings real support to Gen Z (and every generation!) every day. Your dedication and heart made this possible.

To our team of researchers, we thank you for your tireless commitment to studying the depths of human consciousness with scientific rigor and reliability. We also wish to acknowledge the pioneering work of Patrick Merlevede, whose development of the Inventory of Work Attitude and Motivation (iWAM) laid the foundation for Marlee's *Motivation Analysis*, instrumental to *The Gen Z at Work Study* research featured in this book.

To everyone who reviewed, read, or gave feedback, whether it was on a sentence, a section, or just the cover design: thank you. Your thoughtfulness made this book sharper and more relevant. We're also deeply grateful to the Gen Z voices whose stories live in these pages. Your honesty helped ground these insights in real life.

And to the thought leaders, futurists, and online communities who helped us stretch our thinking, thank you for sharing your ideas and your vision. Your collective momentum fueled the questions, conversations, and possibilities that shaped this book.

And finally, to our incredible Marlee community of individuals, teams, organizations, investors, partners, research participants and coaches: we thank you for walking ahead of the pack—with purpose, and with vision. You've been more than early adopters. You've been torchbearers for a future where every person, team, and generation has the chance to thrive.

About the Authors

About Michelle Duval

Michelle Duval has dedicated more than two decades to unlocking human potential—not only as a coach, but by helping to *create* the very fields that guide it today. Widely recognized as a pioneer of coaching science, she co-developed models and handbooks that shaped modern coaching psychology and has trained professionals in more than 60 countries.

Her research has been equally groundbreaking: from exploring neurodiversity and generational change to leading the world's first long-term peer-reviewed study into why some founders scale while others fail. Her work has redefined how entrepreneurial success is understood.

In 2019, Michelle led her team to develop original predictive data and linguistic models to power the earliest conversational AI coach—years before ChatGPT brought AI into everyday life. These innovations became the foundation of *Marlee*, the AI collaboration and performance operating system now supporting teams in more than 95,000 organizations worldwide, including Google, the United Nations, Disney, Canva, and Apple.

Through it all, Michelle's thread of purpose has remained the same: coaching some of the world's most influential culture shapers—scientists, Academy Award–winning storytellers, Olympic athletes, and founders of transformative technology companies—alongside countless parents and everyday humans unfurling their own unique life journey.

Her mission continues to unfold with one clear aim: to help unlock the next evolution of humanity, and to build a sustainable future where every person has the chance to thrive.

About Dan Negroni

Dan Negroni is a globally recognized executive coach, keynote speaker, and leadership educator who helps people and companies unlock their full potential. As the founder and CEO of Launchbox, he has coached leaders across Fortune 1000 companies, startups, and high-growth teams—bridging the generational gap between seasoned executives and emerging Gen Z talent.

With more than 30 years of experience as a CEO, attorney, and sales leader, Dan brings real-world grit to his work. His high-energy, no-nonsense approach has helped companies grow by more than a billion dollars cumulatively. He is also the author of the Amazon bestseller *Chasing Relevance: 6 Steps to Understand, Engage, and Maximize Next-Generation Leaders in the Workplace*.

As a father of Gen Z kids, Dan has seen firsthand how this generation works, thinks, and challenges the status quo. Beyond the boardroom, he teaches business and human skills at California State University, San Marcos, equipping students with the tools to thrive in today's fast-moving Workverse. Whether you're a student, new professional, or team leader, his mission is the same: help you activate your potential, build authentic connections, and lead with impact.

AI Coach Marlee

The third co-author of this book is Marlee, an AI coach created by Michelle Duval and the Marlee team, built on more than 25 years of research into human motivation and performance. At its core is the world's largest dataset on human motivation—16 billion data points that reveal how people work, collaborate, and thrive. Coach Marlee was designed to make the kind of elite coaching once reserved for a few accessible to everyone, anywhere, anytime.

Think of Coach Marlee as your personal coach. With Marlee's technology, you can:

- Access AI coaching programs designed for more than 1,000 different goal types: from leadership to collaboration to personal growth.

- *Ask Marlee* for instant guidance on questions like "What motivates my teammate?" or "How do I convince my manager?"

- Explore interactive *Boards* that map your unique motivations and compare them to your team, your generation, or even global success benchmarks.

This kind of support used to cost hundreds to thousands of dollars per hour and was only available to an elite few. Now, it's in your pocket.

Throughout this book, you'll see reflections and prompts from Coach Marlee: questions designed to help you personalize insights and take action. Behind the scenes is the full Marlee technology; in these pages, Coach Marlee is your guide, challenging your assumptions, encouraging your growth, and helping you design a work life where you can uniquely thrive.

About The Gen Z at Work Study

This book is grounded in insights from *Unlocking Gen Z at Work: A Generational Impact Study* 2024—Marlee's 23-year global research initiative exploring how work motivations have evolved across generations.

The study draws from data on more than 395,000 professionals across 159 countries, including 81,746 Gen Z participants. The findings reveal a major shift in how Gen Z approaches work, from communication and decision-making to what drives motivation, how to boost collaboration, and how to equip Gen Z for success while evolving your workplace to support them.

These insights offer a powerful lens for understanding generational change at work.

Explore the full report at:
https://getmarlee.com/research-study/unlocking-gen-z-study

Endnotes

Chapter 2

1. Manyika, James, et al. 2017. "Jobs Lost, Jobs Gained: What the Future of Work Will Mean for Jobs, Skills, and Wages." Mckinsey.com. McKinsey Global Institute. November 28, 2017. https://www.mckinsey.com/featured-insights/future-of-work/jobs-lost-jobs-gained-what-the-future-of-work-will-mean-for-jobs-skills-and-wages.

2. World Economic Forum. 2025. "The Future of Jobs Report 2025." https://www.weforum.org/publications/the-future-of-jobs-report-2025.

3. Egan, Mark, et al. 2025. "AI-Assisted vs Human-Only Evidence Review: Results from a Comparative Study." Gov.uk. April 23, 2025. https://www.gov.uk/government/publications/ai-assisted-vs-human-only-evidence-review/ai-assisted-vs-human-only-evidence-review-results-from-a-comparative-study.

4. Cai, Kenrick. 2024. "AI's Most Promising Startups Are Getting Younger and Leaner." Forbes Australia. April 11, 2024. https://www.forbes.com.au/news/innovation/ai-50-the-top-artificial-intelligence-startups.

5. Bick, Alexander, et al. 2024. "The Rapid Adoption of Generative AI." September 23, 2024. https://www.stlouisfed.org/on-the-economy/2024/sep/rapid-adoption-generative-ai.

6. Lin, Luona, and Kim Parker. 2025. "3. Workers' Experience with AI Chatbots in Their Jobs." Pew Research Center. February 25, 2025. https://www.pewresearch.org/social-trends/2025/02/25/workers-experience-with-ai-chatbots-in-their-jobs.

7. Journalism University. 2024. "Gutenberg's Legacy: How the Printing

Revolution Changed the World." Journalism & Mass Communication Hub (blog). January 11, 2024. https://journalism.university/media-and-society/gutenbergs-legacy-printing-revolution-impact.

8. Apple. 2023. "App Store Developers Generated $1.1 Trillion in Total Billings and Sales in the App Store Ecosystem in 2022." Apple Newsroom. May 31, 2023. https://www.apple.com/newsroom/2023/05/developers-generated-one-point-one-trillion-in-the-app-store-ecosystem-in-2022.

Chapter 3

9. Sudina Search. 2025. "The average length of a job by generation: A look at workforce trends." Linkedin.com. February 19, 2025. https://www.linkedin.com/pulse/average-length-job-generation-look-workforce-trends-sudina-search-r4wqf.

10. Confino, Paolo. 2023. "Many Gen Zers Have a Full-Time Job and a Side Hustle, Partly Because They're Wary of Getting Burned by Their Employers: 'They've Seen It Happen to Their Parents, to Millennials.'" Fortune. September 27, 2023. https://fortune.com/2023/09/27/why-does-gen-z-have-side-hustles.

11. Baron, Matt. 2025. "$600,000 NSF Grant to Explore Brain-to-Brain Communication Potential." NIU Newsroom. February 5, 2025. https://newsroom.niu.edu/600000-nsf-grant-to-explore-brain-to-brain-communication-potential/.

12. Mullin, Emily. 2025. "Elon Musk's Neuralink Files to Trademark 'Telepathy.'" Wired., March 7, 2025. https://www.wired.com/story/elon-musks-neuralink-files-trademark-telepathy/.

13. Leach, Noa. 2024. "'Nobody Thought It Was Possible': Quantum Teleportation Is Here." BBC Science Focus Magazine. December 20, 2024. https://www.sciencefocus.com/news/impossible-quantum-teleportation.

14. "McKinsey: Generative AI Could Automate Almost 50% of All Working Hours in Europe and US by 2035; Development Means 12 Million Professionals in Both Regions Will Have to Change Jobs in Medium Term, but Demand Will Increase for Professionals in STEM, Health." 2024. Industry Intelligence Inc. July 10, 2024. https://www.industryintel.com/news/mckinsey-generative-ai-could-automate-almost-50-of-all-working-hours-in-europe-and-us-by-2035-development-means-12-million-professionals-in-both-regions-will-have-to-change-jobs-in-medium-term-but-demand-will-increase-for-professionals-in-stem-health-NDAxNjI0LDEyNiwxNjQyN-zI3MTY0ODA.

15. "LinkedIn Founder Feels That 9-to-5 Jobs Will Become a Relic of the Past by 2034!" 2024. Economic Times. July 25, 2024. https://economictimes.indiatimes.com/magazines/panache/linkedin-founder-feels-that-9-to-5-jobs-will-become-a-relic-of-the-past-by-2034/articleshow/112022272.cms.

16. Mearian, Lucas. 2025. "Freelancers Now Represent More than One in Four US Workers." Computerworld. April 23, 2025. https://www.computerworld.com/article/3968698/freelancers-now-represent-more-than-one-in-four-us-workers.html.

Chapter 4

17. Deloitte. 2024. "2024 Gen Z and Millennial Survey: Living and Working with Purpose in a Transforming World." Deloitte.com. 2024. https://www.deloitte.com/content/dam/assets-shared/docs/campaigns/2024/deloitte-2024-genz-millennial-survey.pdf.

18. ETS. 2025. "2025 ETS Human Progress Report." n.d. Ets.org. https://www.ets.org/human-progress-report.html.

Chapter 5

19. Wikipedia contributors. 2025. "Krishna Bharat." Wikipedia, The Free Encyclopedia. July 2, 2025. https://en.wikipedia.org/w/index.

php?title=Krishna_Bharat&oldid=1298433134.

20. Anderson, Charlotte. 2025. "4 Ways Canva Is Designing Engaging, Inclusive People." HRM Online. January 24, 2025. https://www.hrmonline.com.au/culture-leadership/canva-designing-engaging-inclusive-people-experiences.

21. Balch, Oliver. 2025. "Mercadona: Good Employment Practices Pay Off." Financial Times., May 21, 2025. https://www.ft.com/content/6081ad94-fb9c-4340-a9ec-97425a14d110.

22. Beauchene, Vinciane, et al. 2024. "AI at Work 2024: Friend and Foe." BCG Global. June 26, 2024. https://www.bcg.com/publications/2024/ai-at-work-friend-foe.

23. "Burnout Report 2025 Reveals Generational Divide in Levels of Stress and Work Absence." 2025. Mental Health UK. January 16, 2025. https://mental-health-uk.org/blog/burnout-report-2025-reveals-generational-divide-in-levels-of-stress-and-work-absence.

24. Chow, Yeekong, et al. 2018. "Limbic Brain Structures and Burnout—A Systematic Review." Advances in Medical Sciences 63 (1): 192–98. https://doi.org/10.1016/j.advms.2017.11.004.

25. Brandstätter, Veronika, Veronika Job, and Beate Schulze. 2016. "Motivational Incongruence and Well-Being at the Workplace: Person-Job Fit, Job Burnout, and Physical Symptoms." Frontiers in Psychology 7: 1153. https://doi.org/10.3389/fpsyg.2016.01153.

26. Davis, Jeffery. 2025. "How the Art and Science of Pausing Boosts Your Well-Being." Psychology Today., April 2, 2025. https://www.psychologytoday.com/us/blog/tracking-wonder/202503/how-the-art-and-science-of-pausing-boosts-your-well-being.

27. Stafford, Joe. 2025. "Report Highlights How Businesses Can Help Tackle Loneliness." www.manchester.ac.uk. University of Manchester. April 30, 2025.

       https://www.manchester.ac.uk/about/news/report-highlights-how-businesses-can-help-tackle-loneliness.

28. "Gig Talent: Transforming Workforce Strategy with High-Skill Talent." 2025. Draup.com. April 23, 2025. https://draup.com/talent/blogs/gig-work-in-2025-from-flexible-talent-to-workforce-strategy.

29. Hussein, Fatima. 2023. "Online Gig Work Is Growing Rapidly, but Workers Lack Job Protections, a World Bank Report Says." AP News. September 7, 2023. https://apnews.com/article/online-gig-workers-labor-employment-world-bank-40b81a789fd5f0f-b366e83f0223d832f.

30. Harvard Business Review. 2024. "Create a Healthy Multigenerational Workplace.", April 9, 2024. https://hbr.org/tip/2024/04/create-a-healthy-multigenerational-workplace.

31. "Gartner Identifies Top Nine Workplace Predictions for CHROs in 2025." 2025. Gartner.com. January 13, 2025. https://www.gartner.com/en/newsroom/press-releases/2025-01-08-gartner-identifies-top-nine-workplace-predictions-for-chros-in-2025.

Chapter 6

32. "Demand Soars for Human Skills in the Age of AI, According to SkyHive by Cornerstone's New Global State of the Skills Economy Report." 2024. n.d. Cornerstoneondemand.com. https://www.cornerstoneondemand.com/company/news-room/press-releases/human-skills-age-of-ai-global-state-of-the-skills-economy-report.

Chapter 9

33. Van Hooft, Edwin A. J., et al. 2021. "Job Search and Employment Success: A Quantitative Review and Future Research Agenda." The Journal of Applied Psychology 106 (5): 674–713. https://doi.org/10.1037/apl0000675.

Chapter 12

34. "Ipsos World Mental Health Day 2024." 2024. Ipsos.com. October 2024. https://www.ipsos.com/sites/default/files/ct/news/documents/2024-10/Ipsos%20World%20Mental%20Health%20Day%202024%20Global%20Charts%20%281%29.pdf.

35. Saraiva, Margarida, and Teresa Nogueiro. 2025. "Perspectives and Realities of Disengagement among Younger Generation Y and Z Workers in Contemporary Work Dynamics." Administrative Sciences 15 (4): 133. https://doi.org/10.3390/admsci15040133.

Chapter 13

36. Reill, Amanda. 2023. "A Simple Way to Make Better Decisions." Harvard Business Review., December 5, 2023. https://hbr.org/2023/12/a-simple-way-to-make-better-decisions.

37. De Smet, Aaron, Gregor Jost, and Leigh Weiss. 2019. "Three Keys to Faster, Better Decisions." Mckinsey.com. McKinsey Quarterly. May 1, 2019. https://www.mckinsey.com/capabilities/people-and-organizational-performance/our-insights/three-keys-to-faster-better-decisions.

Chapter 14

38. Alliance for Lifetime Income. n.d. "Welcome to the Peak 65® Zone – A New Chapter in America's Retirement Landscape." Protected Income. https://www.protectedincome.org/peak65/.

39. Franzino, Michael, et al. 2018. "The $8.5 Trillion Talent Shortage." Kornferry.com. Korn Ferry. May 9, 2018. https://www.kornferry.com/insights/this-week-in-leadership/talent-crunch-future-of-work.

40. National Research Council, Division of Behavioral and Social Sciences and Education, Commission on Behavioral and Social Sciences and Education, and Committee on Techniques for the Enhancement of Human Performance. 1994.

Learning, Remembering, Believing: Enhancing Human Performance. Edited by Daniel Druckman and Robert A. Bjork. Washington, D.C., DC: National Academies Press.

www.ingramcontent.com/pod-product-compliance
Lightning Source LLC
Chambersburg PA
CBHW020514080526
44583CB00013B/601